D0119662

TRADITIONAL

SOUPS

TRADITIONAL

SOUPS

Eve Parker

AURA

This revised edition published in 2013
by Baker & Taylor (UK) Limited,
Bicester, Oxfordshire

Copyright © 2012 Arcturus Publishing Limited
26/27 Bickels Yard, 151–153 Bermondsey Street
London SE1 3HA

All rights reserved. No part of this publication may be reproduced,
stored in a retrieval system, or transmitted, in any form or by any
means, electronic, mechanical, photocopying, recording or otherwise,
without prior written permission in accordance with the provisions
of the Copyright Act 1956 (as amended). Any person or persons
who do any unauthorised act in relation to this publication may
be liable to criminal prosecution and civil claims for damages.

ISBN: 978-1-90723-125-4
AD002227EN

Printed in China

CONTENTS

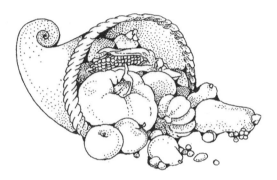

INTRODUCTION

There are many varieties of soup, from the 'ribsticker' with chunky meat and vegetables which is an entire meal in itself, to the refined, glossy consommé which provides an appetizer to a *haute cuisine* experience. While supermarkets sell a huge range of soups, making your own is very satisfying and allows you to pick the very best ingredients.

There is nothing more satisfying than a steaming bowl of soup after a long hike in cold weather, or as a much-needed pick-me-up after a bout of illness. Even when your appetite has largely left you, soup still seems to slip down with ease. In fact, soups are so easy to digest that they have been prescribed for the infirm since time immemorial.

THE HISTORY OF SOUP

No one knows when soup was first invented, but the trick of putting many ingredients into one pot and cooking them slowly until the flavours mingle together has been popular for centuries. Favourite soups evolved around the world, their style depending upon the climate and the local ingredients that were available – for example gazpacho in Spain, borscht in Russia, onion soup in France, minestrone in Italy, chowder in New England, won ton in China and, of course, the classic tomato soup in Britain. Variations on soup such as broth, bouillon and consommé also became fashionable in restaurants in the West and still remain popular today.

The word 'soup' derives from sop, or sup, which was the piece of bread that was either dunked into soup or onto which soup was poured. Until this term came into general usage, soup was generally referred to as broth or pottage and was customarily served with meat or vegetable dishes. Over time, soup came to be regarded as a dish in its own right and it became fashionable to serve it on its own.

By the early 18th century, soup was served as a first course in wealthier households and as a main meal for those with meagre earnings. For invalids, ingredients such as beaten egg, barley and emmer gruel were added to any available vegetables, together with medicinal herbs and spices to aid recovery.

Later, canned or dehydrated in packet form, soup was a convenient food used by the military, by pioneers as their wagon trains crossed the open plains and by weary travellers when there was no chance of a rest or a full meal for miles.

Early 18th-century recipes have been discovered for soups which contain a wide variety of meat, poultry, game, fish, vegetables and grains. In modern times, with foods and spices from all over the world easily available, the choice of ingredients is even wider and the the more you experiment the more varieties of soup you can produce. You will quickly learn which flavours complement one another and which don't really work.

As technology advanced, ways of mass-producing and preserving soup were refined. Today we can buy soup ready prepared in cans and cartons or dried in packets. There are instant soups that just need the addition of boiling water and freeze-dried soups that simply need soaking before eating. Convenient, yes – but the original fresh flavour can be lost, together with many of the nutritional health benefits gained from using totally fresh ingredients.

THE IMPORTANCE OF STOCK

The secret of a good soup, whether meat, fish or vegetable, is a good stock and for that reason the first section in this book, Getting Started, contains basic information and stock recipes (see pp.10–15). Once you have tasted your own homemade soup you will probably want to make it on a regular basis, in which case you will always need to have a batch of stock handy. The best way to achieve this is to make a large quantity and place some in the freezer so that it's ready at a moment's notice.

TYPES OF SOUP

Soups come in a range of different textures and flavours, depending on the process and the ingredients used. For example, a broth or clear soup

is made from a clear stock foundation. A cream soup is puréed after cooking to give it a rich, velvety texture; it is often enhanced by the addition of cream. A chowder is a rich soup, often thickened with crackers and usually containing diced potato and cream.

Bisque – often considered to be one of the luxury soups – is another type of thick, rich soup generally made from game, fish or seafood. Hearty soups, as the name implies, are almost like a stew – all the ingredients are chopped and left whole as opposed to being blended. These soups are a substantial meal in themselves.

Whichever type of soup you choose to make, it is important that all the ingredients are as fresh as possible. It is no good thinking you can use up some old vegetables that have become wrinkled with time, because you will only be disappointed with the end result.

PART 1

GETTING STARTED

Making soups is surprisingly easy, as it requires very little equipment and just a few basic skills. Whether the soup is clear, chilled, creamy or chunky, the methods of cooking are similar; just follow the recipes carefully to get the best results.

LEARNING THE BASICS

This section is a guide on how to make stocks. It tells you what equipment you will need and describes the basic techniques required to make a variety of soups.

MAKING BASIC STOCKS

The basic requirement for a delicious soup is a good-quality foundation stock. You will need four different types of stock – meat, chicken, vegetable and fish. You will discover that these stocks are used repeatedly throughout this book.

The aim of making a stock is to draw the goodness from the ingredients used into the liquid. Any seasoning should be kept to a minimum so that it can be adjusted in the final stages of the soup recipe. Stocks should not be flavoured with herbs as this could interfere with the final flavour of the soup. You also need to be meticulous when it comes to skimming off excess fat, as you don't want to end up with a greasy broth!

If you cook regularly you probably already have a supply of stocks, but if you are starting out and want to try some simple soup recipes you need to get into the habit of keeping meat and poultry bones to make stock. Once you have tasted the flavour of homemade stock you will never again want to buy

those artificially flavoured stock cubes found in abundance on supermarket shelves.

All stocks contain three vegetables – onion, carrot and celery – and a varied range of other ingredients. Here are a few general guidelines:

- Always start with cold water when making stock.

- Add no more water than is sufficient to cover the ingredients in the pan or the end result will be insipid.

- A stock should never be kept at the boil. Just bring the liquid to a fast boil, then immediately reduce it to a simmer.

- Regularly remove any scum from the surface, using a slotted spoon.

- Don't add a lot of seasoning to a stock – if you want to enrich the flavour, boil the stock rapidly after it has been strained to reduce the amount of liquid.

- When straining the stock through a sieve, leave it to drip naturally – don't be tempted to press the cooked ingredients to extract extra liquid.

- Chill the stock rapidly after it is made and remove any fat from the surface once it is cold.

- If you are making a brown stock, roast the bones before adding them to the pan with the vegetables.

Most good chefs have their own version of what they believe to be the perfect stock, but the ones on the following pages are a good guide on how to prepare them and what ingredients to use. You may like to adjust them to suit your own tastes, but remember not to add any strong flavours because they may conflict with other ingredients when it comes to making soups.

CHICKEN STOCK

INGREDIENTS *Makes 1.4 litres/*
2¹/₂ pints
1.8kg/4lb chicken carcass
1 large onion, quartered
1 carrot, roughly chopped
1 celery stick, roughly chopped
1 bay leaf
6 white peppercorns

METHOD
1. Place the chicken carcass in a
large saucepan and cover with
cold water. Bring to the boil then
reduce the heat immediately and
simmer gently for 1 hour, with
the lid on.
2. Remove any scum from the
surface and lift the chicken
from the pot. Allow it to cool,
then remove any flesh from the
carcass and keep it for using in

another recipe. Return the bones
to the pot containing the cooking
liquid and add the onion, carrot,
celery, bay leaf and peppercorns.
Bring back to the boil and then
simmer gently for 3–4 hours with
the lid on.
3. Turn off the heat, remove any
scum and allow the stock to cool
for 10 minutes. Pour it through
a fine-meshed sieve over a
clean bowl and leave to drain
until there is no more liquid
dripping through.
4. Chill the stock in the fridge
and, when cold, remove any fat
that may have formed on the
surface. Keep in the fridge for
3 days; alternatively, freeze in
ice-cube trays so that you always
have stock cubes to hand.

BEEF STOCK

INGREDIENTS *Makes 2 litres/ 3¹/₂ pints*

2kg/4½lb beef marrowbones, chopped into manageable-sized pieces

2 onions, quartered, skins left on

3.4 litres/6 pints water

2 leeks, roughly chopped

2 carrots, roughly chopped

1 celery stick, including leaves, roughly chopped

1 large tomato, roughly chopped

6 black peppercorns

bouquet garni of fresh parsley, sage and thyme

METHOD

1. Preheat the oven to 200°C/400°F/gas mark 6.

2. Place the marrowbones on a baking tray and add the quartered onion. Pour 1cm/½in water into the baking tray and roast in the oven for 40–45 minutes.

3. Place a large saucepan on the hob, add the water and bring it to simmering point. Add the bones and onion from the oven, scraping any brown bits from the base of the baking tray. Add the leeks, carrots, celery, tomato, peppercorns and bouquet garni.

4. Gently simmer the stock, covered, for 6 hours, skimming any scum from the surface from time to time.

5. At the end of the cooking time, strain the stock through a fine sieve into a bowl and discard the bones and vegetables left behind.

6. Return the strained stock to a clean saucepan and bring the mixture to a gentle boil. Cook, uncovered, until the liquid has reduced by half – this should take about 1–1½ hours. The more you reduce the stock the more intense the flavour will be.

7. Chill the stock in the fridge and, once cold, remove any fat that has formed on the surface. Use within 3 days or freeze.

VEGETABLE STOCK

INGREDIENTS *Makes 900ml/1¹/₂ pints*
1 tbsp olive oil
2 onions, chopped
2 carrots, chopped
2 celery sticks, chopped
6 cherry tomatoes, halved
1 garlic clove, crushed
12 button mushrooms, sliced
6 white peppercorns
bouquet garni of fresh thyme,
   parsley and bay leaf
1.2 litres/2 pints cold water

METHOD

1. Heat the olive oil in a large saucepan over a medium heat. Add the onion, carrot and celery and cook until they are soft and starting to go brown.

2. Add the remaining ingredients, bring to a gentle simmer and cook gently for 1–1½ hours, covered. When the cooking time is up, remove the saucepan from the heat and allow to cool for 10 minutes.

3. Strain the stock through a fine sieve, pressing the vegetables with the back of a spoon to extract the last bit of liquid (although this is not recommended for other stocks, vegetable stock is the exception). Discard any remaining solids, cool quickly and chill in the refrigerator. Remove any fat from the surface and use within 3 days or freeze immediately.

FISH STOCK

INGREDIENTS *Makes 900ml/1¹/₂ pints*

1 tbsp olive oil

1 onion, chopped

1 carrot, chopped

2 celery sticks, chopped

1 leek, thinly sliced

250ml/8fl oz dry white wine

1.35kg/3lb white fish bones and
    heads and prawn heads (do
    not use oily fish)

bouquet garni of fresh parsley,
    thyme and bay leaves

1 garlic clove, crushed

6 button mushrooms, sliced

1.2 litres/2 pints cold water

METHOD

1. Heat the olive oil in a frying pan over a medium heat. Add the onion, carrot, celery and leek and cook until they are soft and starting to go brown.

2. Pour the wine into a large saucepan and cook over a high heat until it has reduced by half. Add the fish and prawn bones and heads and the sautéed vegetables from the frying pan. Add the bouquet garni, crushed garlic, mushrooms and water, making sure there is sufficient to cover all the ingredients.

3. Bring the stock to a simmer and cook for 40 minutes. It is important not to boil fish stock because this will make it cloudy. Keep skimming the scum from the surface and at the end of the cooking time strain through a fine mesh sieve with a piece of cheesecloth placed inside. Leave it to drain over a clean bowl and discard anything left in the sieve.

4. Cool rapidly then chill in the refrigerator. Once cold, remove any fat that has formed on the surface. Use within 3 days or freeze immediately.

EQUIPMENT & TECHNIQUES

You do not need any special equipment to make soups, just a few items that you probably already have in your kitchen. Below is a list of items that will definitely make your life easier when cooking up delicious soups.

LARGE SAUCEPAN OR STOCKPOT

By far the most important piece of equipment you will need is a large saucepan or stockpot in which to cook the soup. Make sure you buy a good-quality, thick-based one that can retain the heat at a gentle simmer – stainless steel is by far the best. Remember that some of the heavier pans can be very difficult to lift once they are full of liquid, so take this into account when you are buying.

SET OF SHARP KNIVES

Another essential for chopping ingredients is a decent set of kitchen knives. Keep your knives sharpened and avoid cutting on marble, glass or slate boards as these can blunt the knives quickly. Collect a range of knives, from a paring knife to a bread knife, so that you have one for every need.

CHOPPING BOARDS

Use wooden or plastic boards and try to keep separate ones for vegetables, meat, poultry and fish. Regardless of the type of cutting boards you choose, they should be washed regularly in hot soapy water and occasionally sterilized with a food-safe disinfectant. Once a board is badly scored, it should be thrown away as the cuts can harbour germs.

BLENDER

A good blender is required in order to make creamy or puréed soups. There are two types of blender to choose from: a hand (or immersion) blender which blends the soup in one batch in the cooking pot; or a larger blender that enables you to vary the texture by blending in batches. Remember to make sure the blender lid is secure and hold a tea towel over the top to protect yourself in case you should be splashed by hot liquid.

BAKING TRAY

You will need at least one baking tray, as some of the recipes require the roasting of meat or vegetables before adding them to the soup.

FRYING PAN

A large frying pan is the ideal for sautéing meat and vegetables before they are added to the soup; a smaller pan may mean doing this in batches.

COLANDER

Colanders always come in handy when you have to wash and drain vegetables. They may also be used for layering vegetables such as aubergines that need to be salted before being cooked.

SIEVE

A sieve with a fine mesh is essential when making soups or stocks as most of them will be need to be strained.

GRATER

You will need a grater for grating vegetables, cheese, fresh root ginger or any other food items that need to be very finely shredded.

MEASURING CUPS AND SPOONS

A set of measuring spoons is useful so that you can reliably judge, say, a 'teaspoon' or a 'half teaspoon'. When using a measuring spoon, level off the ingredients with the blade of a knife. Measuring cups are also useful, especially if you are following an American recipe as they will save you having to convert from cup measurements to imperial or metric equivalents.

SCALES

You will need a set of scales for weighing out ingredients. Digital ones are probably the easiest type to use and can be operated in either metric or imperial. If you are weighing something in a bowl, remember to put the reading back to zero with the bowl on the scales before adding the ingredients.

MIXING BOWLS

A couple of mixing bowls will also be useful because you may have to blend certain ingredients together before adding to the soup. For example, dumplings will need to be prepared in a bowl before adding at the last stage of cooking.

LARGE SPOONS OR LADLES

You will need large spoons for stirring and ladles for transferring hot soup into a blender and into serving bowls.

TECHNIQUES

There are no complicated techniques to learn, nor is there a set standard to making soups. Some soups may require you to sauté the vegetables first, others may require you to make a purée, while others may need straining to achieve a clear broth. Each recipe will guide you as to the best way to prepare and cook the ingredients.

You will notice that there are no guidelines on how much salt and pepper to add to a recipe. This will vary according to personal taste. For this reason, a soup should be seasoned at the end of the cooking time to suit the individual's palate.

Fresh herbs add more flavour than dried ones, but if you want to use dried herbs remember to halve the amount suggested for fresh. Always grind your own spices if possible.

Make sure you have all the ingredients before you start a recipe and add your own touches once you become confident.

PART 2

CREAM SOUPS

*All soups are comforting, but somehow
cream soups, with their velvety texture, are
just that little bit more so. A cream soup
is filling enough for lunch with some
crusty bread or perfect as a starter
for a dinner party.*

MAKING CREAM SOUPS

If you enjoy eating soup, you will know there is a wide choice of cream soups in cans and cartons. However, once you have made your own you will be reluctant to return to the ready-made variety, as the home-made version is far superior.

A cream soup is smooth in texture as it has been puréed or blended at the end of the cooking period. This in itself gives the soup a wonderful texture. To make it even more delicious, the addition of cream or milk gives it that final luxurious flavour and silky consistency.

In most recipes the basis of a cream soup is a vegetable purée. To obtain a depth of flavour, the vegetables are usually sautéed first in either oil or butter or a mixture of both and then cooked slowly in a stock flavoured with herbs or spices.

Some cream soups require thickening slightly and this can be done using either a roux or a little cornflour mixed with a small amount of water. Making a roux may sound complicated, but it simply depends on combining equal amounts of butter and plain flour. The butter is melted and then the flour is added and cooked a little so that it starts to lose its raw taste. A roux has a dual purpose in soup making as it not only thickens a cream soup but also prevents the milk and cream from separating.

For a really silky texture the soup can be thickened using a mixture of egg yolks and cream, but you need to heat the mixture slowly otherwise you risk the eggs scrambling.

The amount of cream you add is really up to you, but remember cream will curdle if you let it boil.

ARTICHOKE SOUP

Jerusalem artichokes have a sweet, nutty flavour. Their unique taste makes the most delicious creamy soup.

INGREDIENTS *Serves 4*

450g/1lb Jerusalem artichokes, peeled and diced
225g/8oz floury potatoes, peeled and diced
60g/2oz unsalted butter
1 onion, finely chopped
1 garlic clove, finely chopped
1 celery stick, finely chopped
1 tsp fresh thyme, leaves only
1 litre/1¾ pints chicken or vegetable stock (see pp.12 and 14)
300ml/10fl oz double cream
salt and black pepper, to taste
freshly chopped parsley or crispy bits of Parma ham, to garnish

METHOD

1. Put the artichokes and potatoes in a bowl and soak them in cold water for 10 minutes to remove excess starch.
2. Melt half the butter in a large saucepan, add the onion, garlic, celery and thyme leaves and cook for 10 minutes, stirring regularly, until the onion softens and starts to brown. Drain the artichokes and potatoes and add to the pan. Cook for a further 10 minutes or until they are starting to brown.
3. Add the stock and slowly bring to the boil. Reduce the heat and gently simmer for 40–45 minutes or until the vegetables are tender.
4. Remove from the heat, leave to cool for 5 minutes then pour into a blender and process until smooth. For a really velvety soup, pass the mixture through a fine sieve after blending.
5. Return the soup to a clean pan, add the cream, season to taste with salt and pepper and heat to serve. Top with parsley or crispy bits of Parma ham.

ASPARAGUS SOUP

As soon as the new-season asparagus tips pop their heads out of the soil, it is time to make this delicious soup.

INGREDIENTS *Serves 4–6*

30g/1oz butter
2 tbsp plain flour
½ tsp salt
¼ tsp freshly ground
    black pepper
½ tsp mustard powder
500ml/16fl oz whole milk
450g/1lb fresh asparagus
salt and freshly ground black
    pepper, to taste

METHOD

1. Start by making a white sauce. Melt the butter in a saucepan over a low heat. Gradually blend in the flour, salt, pepper and mustard powder, stirring until it starts to come away from the sides of the pan. Warm the milk and gradually add to the roux, stirring constantly, until the mixture thickens and begins to bubble. Remove from the heat and put to one side.

2. Wash the asparagus and break off any woody ends. Cut into 1cm/½in pieces and cook for 5 minutes in a small amount of boiling water. Drain, reserving the cooking liquid. Keep a few asparagus tips as garnish.

3. Put the remaining asparagus in a blender and process until smooth.

4. Add boiling water to the asparagus cooking water until you have 250ml/8fl oz, then add the water and the puréed asparagus to the white sauce in the other saucepan.

5. Check the seasoning then heat thoroughly, without boiling, before serving.

6. Serve in individual bowls with a couple of asparagus tips on top.

BABY BROAD BEAN & MINT SOUP

The pale green colour of this soup looks amazing flecked with the darker green chopped fresh mint.

INGREDIENTS *Serves 4*

450g/1lb baby broad beans, shelled

30g/1oz unsalted butter

1 small onion, chopped

1 celery stick, finely chopped

2 tbsp pudding rice

1 litre/1¾ pints hot chicken or vegetable stock (see pp.12 and 14)

salt and freshly ground black pepper, to taste

1 tbsp fresh mint leaves, finely chopped

90ml/3fl oz plain yogurt

fresh mint leaves and cayenne pepper, to serve

METHOD

1. Blanch the broad beans in boiling water for 2 minutes, then allow to cool and pop the beans out of their skins. Set to one side.

2. Heat the butter in a heavy-based saucepan and add the onion and celery. Cook over a low heat for about 10 minutes or until they are soft but not brown.

3. Add the rice and cook for one more minute.

4. Add the broad beans and hot stock and bring to the boil. Reduce the heat immediately to a slow simmer and cook for about 10–15 minutes or until the rice is cooked.

5. Allow the soup to cool slightly, then pour into a blender and process in batches until the soup is smooth.

6. Return the soup to a clean saucepan and reheat. Season to taste with salt and pepper. Just prior to serving, stir in the chopped mint and yogurt, but do not reheat. Serve with a couple of fresh mint leaves and a dash of cayenne pepper.

BEETROOT SOUP

Beetroot's natural sweetness and vibrant colour make this velvety soup a real winner!

INGREDIENTS *Serves 4*
30g/1oz unsalted butter
3 beetroots, chopped
1 potato, chopped
2 shallots, chopped
1 garlic clove, crushed
1 tbsp red wine vinegar
750ml/1¼ pints hot vegetable
   stock (see p.14)
1 bay leaf
salt and freshly ground black
   pepper, to taste
60g/2oz Gruyère cheese, grated

TO GARNISH:
90ml/3fl oz double cream
1 tbsp finely chopped
   fresh parsley

METHOD
1. Melt the butter in a large saucepan over a medium heat. Add the chopped beetroot, potato, shallots and garlic and cook for 10 minutes or until the onion is soft. Add the vinegar, hot vegetable stock and bay leaf and simmer for about 20 minutes or until the vegetables are really tender.

2. Remove from the heat and take out the bay leaf. Transfer the soup to a blender and process until smooth.

3. Pass the soup through a fine sieve, then return it to a clean saucepan and season with salt and pepper. Gently reheat and add the Gruyère cheese, which should melt and blend with the soup.

4. Once the soup is heated through, pour into individual bowls and swirl the cream over the surface so that you have a spiral pattern. Sprinkle with the chopped parsley and serve immediately.

BROCCOLI & STILTON SOUP

The tangy flavour of the Stilton cheese really brings out the flavour of the broccoli. This deliciously warming soup is great for a quick lunch or a chilly evening supper.

INGREDIENTS *Serves 4*

30g/1oz butter

225g/8oz broccoli florets, roughly chopped

1 potato, peeled and cut into cubes

1 onion, chopped

1 tbsp plain flour

400ml/14fl oz chicken or vegetable stock (see pp.12 and 14)

60g/2oz Stilton cheese

270ml/9fl oz milk

60ml/2fl oz double cream

salt and freshly ground black pepper, to taste

METHOD

1. Melt the butter in a large frying pan over a medium heat and add the broccoli, potato and onion. Cover the pan and cook for about 10 minutes or until the vegetables are soft. Stir from time to time to prevent them sticking.

2. Mix the flour with a little of the stock and add this with the remaining stock to the pan. Stir thoroughly, cover the pan again, and simmer gently for 35 minutes.

3. Crumble the cheese into small pieces and add to the soup along with the milk. Stir to combine and turn up the heat slightly until the mixture is simmering, but do not allow it to boil. Cook for 5 minutes to allow the cheese to melt.

4. Transfer to a blender and process the soup until it is thick and smooth.

5. Just before serving, add the cream and season with salt and pepper. Reheat but do not allow the soup to boil otherwise you risk the cream curdling.

BUTTERNUT & GINGER SOUP

The colour alone makes this soup very inviting, as butternut squash
does not lose its wonderful golden hue, even when cooked.

INGREDIENTS *Serves 4*
30g/1oz unsalted butter
2 leeks, sliced into rounds
700g/1lb 8oz butternut squash,
    peeled, deseeded and cut
    into chunks
5cm/2in fresh root ginger, grated
500ml/16fl oz vegetable stock
    (see p.14)
1 bouquet garni made up of fresh
    parsley, thyme and rosemary
120ml/4fl oz double cream
½ tsp hot smoked paprika
salt and freshly ground black
    pepper, to taste

METHOD
1. Melt the butter in a large
saucepan over a medium heat.
Add the leeks and sauté until
they are soft.
2. Add the butternut squash,
grated ginger, vegetable stock
and bouquet garni and bring
to the boil. Reduce the heat to a
gentle simmer, cover with a lid
and cook for 25–30 minutes or
until the squash is really soft.
3. Remove from the heat and take
out the bouquet garni. Transfer
the soup to a blender and
process until it is really smooth
and free of lumps.
4. Return the soup to a clean
saucepan, add the cream and
paprika and season to taste
with salt and pepper. Heat
before serving, but do not allow
the soup to boil.

CARROT & ORANGE SOUP

Freshly squeezed orange juice adds extra zing to this classic soup, which is excellent served with some warm, crusty bread.

INGREDIENTS *Serves 4*
30g/1oz unsalted butter
1 large onion, finely chopped
450g/1lb carrots, chopped
1 tbsp plain flour
600ml/1 pint hot vegetable stock
    (see p.14)
1 sprig of mint
the grated zest and juice of
    an orange
½ tsp ground ginger
60ml/2fl oz natural Greek yogurt
salt and freshly ground black
    pepper, to taste
freshly chopped coriander and
    extra yogurt, to garnish

METHOD
1. Melt the butter in a large saucepan and add the chopped onion. Cook gently until it is softened but not browned.
2. Add the chopped carrots to the pan and cook for a minute.

Stir in the flour and cook for a further minute.
3. Pour in the hot vegetable stock and add the mint, grated orange zest and ginger. Bring to the boil, then reduce the heat and simmer gently, covered, for 15 minutes or until the carrots are tender.
4. Remove the sprig of mint, pour the soup into a blender and process until smooth. Pour the blended soup into a clean saucepan, add the orange juice and yogurt and season to taste with salt and pepper. Give it a good stir then heat gently.
5. Serve the soup garnished with an extra dollop of yogurt and some chopped coriander.

CAULIFLOWER & CHEESE SOUP

This ultra-creamy soup will quickly chase away any winter blues with its blend of vegetables and Gruyère cheese.

INGREDIENTS *Serves 6*

1 cauliflower head, broken into
    small florets
75g/2½oz unsalted butter
1 leek, sliced into rounds
1 onion, finely chopped
1 carrot, chopped
1 tsp dried tarragon
½ tsp dried thyme
4 tbsp plain flour
200ml/7fl oz dry white wine
1.2 litres/2 pints vegetable stock
    (see p.14)
250ml/8fl oz semi-skimmed milk
250ml/8fl oz double cream
250g/9oz Gruyère cheese, grated
salt and freshly ground black
    pepper, to taste
croutons, to garnish

METHOD

1. Steam the cauliflower florets until they are fairly soft.
2. Melt the butter in a large saucepan over a medium heat and add the leek, onion and carrot. Cook for 10 minutes, stirring occasionally, until the vegetables are beginning to soften.
3. Stir in the tarragon and thyme and cook for 1 minute. Stir in the flour and cook for a further minute. Reduce the heat and gradually stir in the wine and vegetable stock. Add the steamed cauliflower and simmer, uncovered, for 30 minutes, giving it an occasional stir.
4. Transfer the soup to a blender in batches and process until smooth. Return to a clean saucepan, stir in the milk, cream and cheese and season to taste with salt and pepper. Gently heat until the cheese has melted.
5. Serve in individual bowls, garnished with croutons.

CELERIAC & ROASTED GARLIC SOUP

This winter vegetable is often overlooked but it makes a wonderful soup, especially with the addition of sweet roasted garlic.

INGREDIENTS *Serves 6*

12 garlic cloves

75g/2½oz unsalted butter, softened

1 onion, finely diced

60g/2oz smoked streaky bacon, finely diced

1 leek, white only, finely sliced

1 celery stick, finely diced

2 sprigs of fresh thyme, leaves only

700g/1lb 8oz celeriac, peeled and finely diced

1 litre/1¾ pints vegetable stock (see p.14)

200ml/7fl oz double cream

salt and white pepper, to taste

METHOD

1. Preheat the oven to 160°C/320°F/gas mark 3.

2. Lay the garlic cloves on a baking tray and cook in the oven for 20 minutes or until soft. As soon as they are cool enough to handle, squeeze each clove out of its skin and set to one side.

3. Melt half the butter in a large saucepan, add the onion and bacon and fry for 5–6 minutes over a medium heat until the onion starts to soften.

4. Add the leek, celery and thyme and fry for a further minute. Add the celeriac and then pour in the stock. Bring to the boil, reduce the heat to a simmer and cook for 15–20 minutes, or until the celeriac is just tender.

5. Pour the soup into a blender, add the roasted garlic and process until you have a purée.

6. Pour the soup back into a clean saucepan, then whisk in the remaining butter and the cream. Season to taste with salt and white pepper and heat gently before serving.

CELERY & LEEK SOUP

Fortify yourself against the winter chill with this warming, almost nutty-flavoured soup.

INGREDIENTS *Serves 4*
30g/1oz unsalted butter
1 large onion, finely chopped
1 large head of celery, trimmed
   and sliced
2 leeks, white parts only, sliced
1 tbsp fresh parsley, chopped
450ml/15fl oz vegetable stock
   (see p.14)
300ml/10fl oz semi-skimmed milk
60ml/2fl oz double cream
salt and freshly ground white
   pepper, to taste
celery leaves, to garnish

METHOD
1. Melt the butter in a large saucepan, add the onion, celery and leek, and cook gently for 10 minutes without browning.
2. Add the chopped parsley and stock and bring to the boil. Reduce the heat, cover, and simmer gently for 25 minutes or until the vegetables are soft.
3. Spoon the soup into a blender and process until you have a smooth purée.
4. Pour the soup into a clean saucepan, add the milk and slowly bring to a simmer, cooking for 5 minutes. Stir in the cream and season to taste with salt and pepper.
5. Ladle into warm soup bowls and garnish with a few celery leaves or extra chopped parsley.

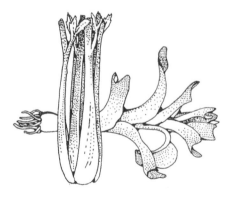

CHICKEN & SWEETCORN SOUP

This lovely variation on cream of chicken soup contains juicy pieces of corn and a hint of sage.

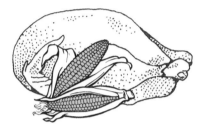

INGREDIENTS *Serves 4*

60g/2oz unsalted butter

60g/2oz spring onions, finely
    shredded

1 leek, white parts only, finely
    shredded

1 tsp dried sage

85g/3oz plain flour

1 litre/1¾ pints hot chicken stock
    (see p.12)

400g/14oz cooked chicken breast,
    cut into fine strips

198g/7oz can sweetcorn, drained

salt and freshly ground black
    pepper, to taste

200ml/7fl oz double cream

METHOD

1. Melt the butter in a large saucepan over a medium heat and add the spring onions, leek and sage. Sweat for 2 minutes, then add the flour and stir to make a roux. Cook gently for a few minutes without allowing it to change colour.

2. Slowly add the hot chicken stock, stirring constantly to stop it from going lumpy. Once it starts to thicken, turn down the heat and simmer for 10 minutes.

3. Add the chicken strips and sweetcorn and season to taste with salt and pepper. Check the consistency and if you feel it is too thick add a little extra chicken stock.

4. Add the cream and reheat gently just before serving.

CREAM OF CHICKEN SOUP

This all-time favourite, flavoured with aromatic tarragon, makes a very special starter.

INGREDIENTS *Serves 4*

30g/1oz unsalted butter

1 small onion, finely chopped

1 garlic clove, crushed

200g/7oz potatoes, peeled and finely chopped

1 leek, white parts only, thinly sliced

2 sprigs of fresh tarragon

750ml/1¼ pints hot chicken stock (see p.12)

100ml/3½fl oz dry white wine

200g/7oz hot roasted skinless chicken breast, cut into small pieces

½ tsp lemon juice

120ml/4fl oz double cream

salt and white pepper, to taste

2 shallots, finely shredded, to garnish

METHOD

1. Heat the butter in a large saucepan over a medium heat. Add the onion and garlic and cook for 5–6 minutes until softened but not browned.

2. Stir in the potatoes, leeks and a sprig of tarragon and cook for a further 15 minutes, covered.

3. Pour in the hot stock and wine and cook for a further 30 minutes.

4. Pour the soup into the blender and add the chicken pieces while they are still hot, along with the lemon juice. Process until the soup is smooth and creamy.

5. Pour the soup into a clean saucepan, add the cream and season to taste with salt and pepper. Reheat gently but do not allow it to boil.

6. Fry the shredded shallots in a very hot pan with a little oil until they are brown and crispy. Sprinkle them over the hot soup together with a little chopped tarragon.

CREAMY CUCUMBER SOUP

While most of us think of cucumber purely as a salad vegetable,
it also makes a lovely soup which can be eaten
either hot or chilled.

INGREDIENTS *Serves 4*

30g/1oz unsalted butter

2 garlic cloves, finely chopped

1 small onion, finely chopped

1 tbsp lemon juice

600g/1lb 5oz cucumber, peeled,
   deseeded and diced

375ml/13fl oz vegetable stock
   (see p.14)

½ tsp cayenne pepper

1 avocado, diced

1 tbsp fresh parsley, finely
   chopped

120ml/4fl oz soured cream

salt and freshly ground black
   pepper, to taste

METHOD

1. Heat the butter in a large
saucepan over a medium heat.
Add the garlic and onion and
cook for 5–6 minutes until just
tender but not browned.

2. Add the lemon juice and cook
for 1 more minute.

3. Add the cucumber, reserving
a little for garnish. Now add the
stock and cayenne pepper and
bring to the boil. Reduce the
heat and simmer gently for 8–10
minutes or until the cucumber
is soft.

4. Transfer the soup to a blender,
add the avocado flesh and
parsley and blend until smooth.

5. If you are serving the soup hot,
return it to a clean saucepan, stir
in the soured cream and season
with salt and pepper. Heat gently
and serve garnished with the
reserved diced cucumber.

6. If you are serving the soup
chilled, do not reheat it – just
put it in the refrigerator for a
couple of hours after adding
the soured cream.

LEEK & PEA SOUP

Sweet yet pungent, leeks make a wonderful soup. In this recipe baby leeks are used so that their flavour does not overpower the delicate taste of the peas.

INGREDIENTS *Serves 4*
30g/1oz unsalted butter
1 onion, finely chopped
6 baby leeks, finely chopped
2 celery sticks, chopped
1 potato, peeled and chopped
1 bunch of fresh thyme
600ml/1 pint hot vegetable stock
    (see p.14)
550g/1¼lb fresh or frozen peas
120ml/4fl oz double cream
salt and freshly ground black
    pepper, to taste
1 tsp truffle-infused oil
1 tsp sugar, or to taste

METHOD
1. Melt the butter in a large saucepan over a medium heat. Add the onion, leeks and celery and sauté for about 10 minutes or until soft but not browned. Add the potato, thyme and vegetable stock and bring to the boil.

2. Reduce the heat and cook, covered, for 10–15 minutes or until the potatoes are soft. Remove from the heat and set on one side.

3. In another saucepan, bring some lightly salted water to the boil and cook the peas for 3–5 minutes. Drain and immediately drop them into iced water so that they do not lose their vibrant colour.

4. Add the peas to the other saucepan and discard the thyme. Pour the soup into a blender and process until you have a smooth purée.

5. Return the soup to a clean saucepan and add the cream, salt and pepper, truffle oil and sugar and warm gently.

LEEK & POTATO SOUP

This is possibly one of the easiest soups to make, and despite its few ingredients it always turns out well. Eaten with plenty of bread, it can make a substantial meal in itself.

INGREDIENTS *Serves 4–6*

30g/1oz unsalted butter

225g/8oz potatoes, peeled and cubed

1 onion, finely chopped

1 garlic clove, crushed

3 leeks, white parts only, thinly sliced

salt and freshly ground black pepper, to taste

1.2 litres/2 pints hot vegetable stock (see p.14)

150ml/5fl oz double cream

snipped chives, to garnish

METHOD

1. Melt the butter in a large saucepan and when it starts to foam, add the potatoes, onion, garlic and leeks and stir until they are coated in the butter. Season with salt and pepper. Place a circle of greaseproof paper over the top of the vegetables to keep the steam in, then cover with the saucepan lid. Cook over a gentle heat for 10 minutes.

2. Discard the greaseproof paper and pour in the vegetable stock. Bring to the boil, then turn down the heat and simmer gently for about 5–6 minutes or until the vegetables are just cooked.

3. Purée the soup in a blender until it is really smooth and then taste and adjust the seasoning if necessary. Add the double cream and reheat gently to serve. If you find the soup is too thick you can always add a little milk or some more stock at this stage.

4. Serve in individual bowls with plenty of snipped chives.

MUSHROOM SOUP

Adding a few dried Portobello mushrooms to this creamy soup
gives a real depth of flavour.

INGREDIENTS *Serves 4*

85g/3oz dried Portobello
   mushrooms
500g/1lb fresh mushrooms
60g/2oz butter
2 onions, chopped
1 garlic clove, crushed
2 tbsp plain flour
1 litre/1¾ pints hot vegetable
   stock (see p.14)
1 bay leaf
120ml/4fl oz double cream
salt and freshly ground black
   pepper, to taste

METHOD

1. Soak the Portobello mushrooms
in hot water for 10 minutes, then
remove from the water and chop.
2. Prepare the fresh mushrooms
by wiping any compost from
the stalks and then chopping the
stalks and tops.
3. Melt the butter in a large
saucepan over medium heat,
add the onions and garlic and
cook for 5 minutes or until they
are soft but not browned.
4. Add the Portobello and fresh
mushrooms to the pan and stir
over a high heat for 3 minutes.
5. Sprinkle in the flour and stir
until the mushrooms are well
coated. Gradually pour in the
hot vegetable stock, stirring
constantly until it is thoroughly
combined, then bring to the boil.
Add the bay leaf, turn down the
heat and cook at a gentle simmer
for 10 minutes.
6. Remove the bay leaf and
allow the soup to cool for a few
minutes. Pour into a blender and
process until really smooth.
7. Pour the soup into a clean pan,
stir in the cream, season, and
reheat gently before serving.

PEA SOUP

This soup is easy to make and is a delicious treat on a chilly winter's evening.

INGREDIENTS *Serves 4*

30g/1oz butter

2 banana shallots, finely chopped

400g/14oz fresh or frozen peas, podded

360ml/12fl oz hot vegetable stock (see p.14)

2 sprigs of fresh mint

150ml/5fl oz double cream

salt and freshly ground black pepper, to taste

METHOD

1. Melt the butter in a large saucepan over medium heat and add the chopped shallots. Cook over a medium heat for 5 minutes or until the shallots have softened but not browned.

2. Add the peas to the saucepan together with the hot stock and mint sprigs and bring to the boil. Turn down the heat and simmer for 5 minutes.

3. Remove the soup from the heat and allow it to cool for a few minutes. Remove the mint sprigs. Pour the soup into a blender and process until you have a smooth paste.

4. Pour the soup into a clean saucepan. Stir in the cream, season to taste with salt and pepper and reheat gently before serving.

If you like a bit of extra zing, add the grated zest of half a lime to the cream before serving.

PEA & HAM SOUP

This recipe is great for using up any leftover pieces of ham – ideal at Christmas when you want something a bit different.

INGREDIENTS *Serves 4*

30g/1oz butter
1 large onion, finely chopped
1 garlic clove, crushed
2 celery sticks, finely chopped
1 large carrot, chopped
450g/1lb dried green split peas
2 sprigs of fresh parsley
1.2 litres/2 pints hot chicken stock
   (see p.12)
225g/8oz cooked ham, chopped
salt and freshly ground black
   pepper, to taste
double cream and chopped
   parsley, to garnish

METHOD

1. Melt the butter in a large saucepan over a medium heat and add the onion. Cook for 5 minutes until soft but not browned. Add the garlic, celery and carrot and cook for a further 3 minutes.
2. Add the split peas and parsley to the saucepan, then pour in the hot stock. Bring to the boil, then turn down the heat and simmer gently for an hour or until the vegetables are soft.
3. Remove the soup from the heat and allow it to cool down for a few minutes. Remove the parsley sprigs. Pour the soup into a blender and process until smooth.
4. Put the soup into a clean saucepan, add the chopped ham and season to taste. Heat thoroughly before serving.
5. Pour into warmed serving bowls and swirl the top of each with double cream. Sprinkle some finely chopped parsley over to finish.

This soup freezes well and, once frozen, will keep for 2 months.

POTATO SOUP

This soup is a comforting classic and the potatoes and leek give it a surprisingly delicate flavour.

INGREDIENTS *Serves 4*

30g/1oz butter

450g/1lb potatoes, peeled and chopped

1 head of celery with leaves, sliced

2 spring onions, chopped

1 leek, white parts only, sliced

2 garlic cloves, crushed

1 litre/1¾ pints hot vegetable stock (see p.14)

4 tbsp crème fraîche

salt and freshly ground black pepper, to taste

2 rashers smoked streaky bacon, diced

60g/2oz Stilton cheese, to garnish

METHOD

1. Melt the butter in a large saucepan over a medium heat. Add the potatoes, celery, spring onions and leek and sauté gently for 5 minutes, or until the

vegetables have started to soften.

2. Add the garlic and hot stock to the pan and bring to the boil. Reduce the heat and simmer gently for 25 minutes.

3. Remove the pan from the heat and allow to cool slightly. Pour the soup into a blender and process until smooth.

4. Return the soup to a clean saucepan, stir in the crème fraîche and season to taste with salt and pepper. Reheat gently.

5. While the soup is warming, fry the bacon until it is brown and crispy.

6. Pour the soup into warmed bowls and top each one with the bacon and some pieces of Stilton, crumbled.

PUMPKIN SOUP

Next time your children ask for a pumpkin lantern at Halloween, don't throw the flesh away – make some creamy soup to warm them up after 'trick or treating'.

INGREDIENTS *Serves 4*

1.8kg/4lb pumpkin
30g/1oz butter
1 large onion, finely chopped
1.2 litres/2 pints hot vegetable
    stock (see p.14)
200ml/7fl oz double cream
salt, pepper and freshly grated
    nutmeg, to taste

METHOD

1. Peel the pumpkin, discard the seeds and chop the flesh into 2.5cm/1in chunks.
2. Melt the butter in a large saucepan over a medium heat. Add the chopped onion and cook for 5–6 minutes until soft but not browned.
3. Add the pumpkin and hot vegetable stock, bring to the boil, then turn down the heat to a gentle simmer. Cover with the lid and cook for about 20 minutes or until the vegetables are soft.
4. Remove the pan from the heat and allow to cool slightly. Pour the soup into a blender and process until smooth and creamy.
5. Pour the soup back into a clean saucepan and add the cream, salt and pepper and nutmeg to taste. Reheat the soup gently before serving.

ROASTED RED PEPPER SOUP

This makes a lovely change from regular cream of tomato soup. The combination of sweet pepper, tomato and onion makes it a winning dish for any occasion.

INGREDIENTS *Serves 4*
4 large sweet red peppers, deseeded and quartered
4 garlic cloves, skin on
1 tsp dried oregano
4 tbsp olive oil
1 large red onion, chopped
6 large tomatoes, skinned, deseeded and chopped
900ml/1½ pints hot vegetable stock (see p.14)
1 tsp sugar
handful of fresh basil leaves, retaining some for garnish
salt and freshly ground black pepper, to taste

METHOD
1. Preheat the oven to 200°C/400°F/gas mark 6.
2. Place the peppers and garlic on a baking tray, sprinkle with the oregano and drizzle with some of the olive oil. Roast for 30–35 minutes or until the pepper skins have started to blister. Put the hot peppers inside a plastic bag and seal. When cool, peel off the skin and chop the flesh.
3. Heat the remaining olive oil in a large pan and fry the onion for 10 minutes or so, until softened. Add the tomatoes, peppers, stock, sugar and a few basil leaves. Squeeze the garlic out of its papery husk into the pan, then cover the pan and bring to the boil. Reduce the heat and simmer for 30 minutes.
4. Process the soup in a blender until smooth and then return it to a clean saucepan and reheat before serving, seasoning with salt and pepper to taste.
5. Serve garnished with a few basil leaves.

ROASTED VEGETABLE SOUP

Roasting the vegetables first gives this soup a sweet, intense flavour. Although this recipe is a little fiddly to make, it is well worth the time and effort.

INGREDIENTS *Serves 6*

1 large onion

225g/8oz carrot

225g/8oz sweet potato, peeled

225g/8oz butternut squash, peeled

225g/8oz sweet red pepper, deseeded

175g/6oz fresh tomatoes, skinned and deseeded

2 tbsp olive oil

2 sprigs of fresh rosemary

1 whole garlic head

1.2 litres/2 pints hot vegetable stock (see p.14)

salt and freshly ground black pepper, to taste

200g/7oz carton Greek-style yogurt, to serve

METHOD

1. Preheat the oven to 150°C/ 300°F/gas mark 2.

2. Chop all the vegetables except the garlic into approximately 5cm/2in pieces so that they are as uniform in size as possible. Toss the vegetable pieces in the olive oil, then arrange them in a single layer on baking trays. Add the rosemary sprigs, then place the baking trays in the oven for about 1½–2 hours.

3. After the first hour of cooking, add the garlic head. At the end of the cooking time the vegetables should be tender and slightly caramelized.

4. Remove the rosemary and place the vegetables in a large saucepan with the hot vegetable stock. Squeeze the garlic out of its papery husks before adding it to the pan. Pour a little stock into the baking trays, scrape and pour the liquid back into the saucepan to get every last bit of goodness from the sticky residue.

5. Bring the mixture to the boil, then reduce the heat and simmer for 15 minutes. Remove the pan from the heat and allow it to cool slightly.

6. Pour the soup in batches into a blender and process until it is really smooth and creamy.

7. Return the soup to a clean saucepan and reheat before serving. Add salt and pepper to taste and serve each bowl of soup with a generous dollop of Greek yogurt.

CHEF'S TIP

You can use any type of vegetables in this soup – you do not have to stick to the ones suggested here. While you are preparing them for the soup, it's a good idea to double the quantity, then you will have enough to serve as a side dish with your main course. Roasted vegetables are delicious drizzled with a little balsamic vinegar.

SPICY SQUASH & CHORIZO SOUP

This soup is for anyone who fancies something a little spicy, yet still wants the comfort of a creamy, luxurious soup.

INGREDIENTS *Serves 4–6*

450g/1lb butternut squash, peeled, deseeded and cut into 2.5cm/1in chunks
3 tbsp olive oil
200g/7oz chorizo, skin removed and cut into 1cm/½in slices
1 onion, finely chopped
1 carrot, diced
1 celery stick, diced
1 garlic clove, finely chopped
1 tsp hot smoked paprika
750ml/1¼ pints hot chicken stock (see p.12)
salt and freshly ground black pepper, to taste

METHOD

1. Preheat the oven to 180°C/350°F/gas mark 4.

2. Lay the prepared butternut squash on a baking tray and drizzle with half the olive oil. Bake in the oven for 20 minutes or until it is soft and just starting to brown.

3. Heat the remaining oil in a large saucepan over medium heat and add the chorizo. Fry gently for 10 minutes or until it has released most of its fat. Remove the chorizo with a slotted spoon and place on some kitchen paper to drain.

4. Drain most of the fat from the saucepan, retaining about 1 tablespoon, then fry the onion for about 10 minutes or until soft. Add the carrot and celery, stir and cover. Cook very gently for 15 minutes, shaking the pan occasionally, until the vegetables are soft.

5. Add the garlic to the pan and cook, uncovered, for a further minute.

6. Stir in the paprika, then add the squash and stir until it is

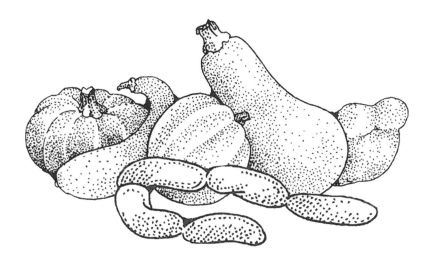

thoroughly mixed with the other vegetables. Pour the hot stock into the saucepan and bring to a gentle simmer. Cook, covered, for 15 minutes.

7. Allow the soup to cool slightly, then transfer it to a blender and purée until it is creamy and smooth.

8. Return the soup to the saucepan and stir in the fried chorizo, reserving a little for garnish. Season the soup to taste with salt and pepper and warm through before serving.

9. Serve in warmed soup bowls. Chop the reserved chorizo very finely and sprinkle it on top of each one.

VARIATION

Chorizo is a Spanish sausage made from fresh pork flavoured with garlic, chilli powder and other spices. It adds a smoky, spicy flavour to this creamy soup. If you like your soup even spicier, try adding a couple of red chillies, deseeded and chopped, when you add the carrot and celery in Step 3.

SPICY RED LENTIL SOUP

Here the mild flavour of lentils is enhanced with spices to make this a warming and comforting soup for winter nights.

INGREDIENTS *Serves 4–6*

1 tbsp olive oil
1 onion, roughly chopped
2 celery sticks, roughly chopped
1 carrot, roughly chopped
1 garlic clove, crushed
1 tsp ground cumin
½ tsp ground coriander
½ tsp hot chilli powder
175g/6oz split red lentils
1.2 litres/2 pints hot vegetable
    stock (see p.14)
400g/14oz can chopped tomatoes
2 bay leaves
2 tsp tomato purée
salt and freshly ground black
    pepper, to taste
4 tbsp Greek-style yogurt,
    to garnish

METHOD

1. Heat the oil in a large saucepan and cook the onion over a low heat for 7–8 minutes or until softened. Add the celery and carrot and cook for a further 3 minutes, stirring. Stir in the garlic, cumin, coriander and chilli powder and cook for another minute.

2. Add the lentils, stock, tomatoes and bay leaves. Bring to the boil, reduce the heat, half cover the pan and simmer for 30 minutes or until the lentils and vegetables are soft.

3. Remove the bay leaves and process the soup in a blender until it is smooth and creamy.

4. Return the soup to a clean pan, stir in the tomato purée, season to taste with salt and pepper and reheat before serving.

5. Garnish each bowl with a dollop of Greek yogurt. For an added treat, fry some chopped onion until it is crispy and golden brown and sprinkle over the top.

SPINACH SOUP

This wonderfully healthy soup contains iron-rich spinach and is a great way to get children to eat one of their five-a-day.

INGREDIENTS *Serves 4*

1 tbsp olive oil, plus extra
    for drizzling
1 onion, finely chopped
2 garlic cloves, finely chopped
1 potato, peeled and diced
200g/7oz fresh spinach leaves
150ml/5fl oz hot vegetable stock
    (see p.14)
75ml/2½fl oz whole milk
60g/2oz butter
salt and freshly ground black
    pepper, to taste
100g/4oz white bread, cut into
    small cubes
grated Parmesan cheese,
    to garnish

METHOD

1. Heat the olive oil in a large saucepan, add the onion and fry for 5 minutes or until softened, but not browned. Add the garlic and potato and cook for a further 2 minutes. Stir in half of the spinach and allow it to wilt in the pan for 2 minutes. Add the hot stock, the milk and half the butter and bring to the boil. Reduce the heat and simmer for 5–6 minutes.

2. Stir in the remaining spinach leaves and cook for a further 2 minutes or until the spinach has wilted.

3. Allow the soup to cool a little before pouring into a blender. Process until smooth.

4. Return the soup to a clean saucepan and heat through before serving.

5. Make croutons by melting the remaining butter in a frying pan and frying the bread cubes until they are golden brown. Spoon the soup into individual bowls and garnish with a few croutons and a generous sprinkling of Parmesan.

SWEET POTATO & LEEK SOUP

Sweet potatoes are a versatile vegetable that can be roasted, mashed or cut into matchsticks and fried for a sweeter version of chips. Blended with leeks, they make a delicious soup.

INGREDIENTS *Serves 4*

1 tbsp extra virgin olive oil
2 large sweet potatoes, peeled and cut into cubes
1 large leek, sliced
2.5cm/1in fresh root ginger, peeled and finely chopped
1 garlic clove, finely chopped
500ml/16fl oz vegetable stock (see p.14)
120ml/4fl oz coconut milk
salt and freshly ground black pepper, to taste
crème fraîche, to serve

METHOD

1. Heat the oil in a large saucepan, add the sweet potato, leek and ginger and sauté gently for 6 minutes until they are softened but not browned.

2. Add the garlic and stir for a couple of minutes until it has softened slightly.

3. Add the vegetable stock and bring to the boil. Turn down the heat and cook at a gentle simmer, covered, for 30 minutes.

4. Pour the soup into a blender, add the coconut milk and process until silky smooth.

5. Return the soup to a clean saucepan, season with salt and pepper to taste, then reheat gently before serving.

6. Serve in warmed soup bowls with a good dollop of crème fraîche in each.

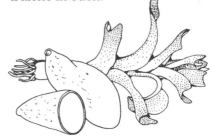

TOMATO & BEETROOT SOUP

Beetroot not only adds an earthy flavour to this soup, it also gives it a vibrant colour, set off by cubes of white feta cheese.

INGREDIENTS *Serves 4*

450g/1lb fresh tomatoes, halved
1 garlic clove, chopped
2 tbsp olive oil
1 onion, finely chopped
450g/1lb beetroot, peeled and
    chopped
750ml/1¼ pints hot vegetable
    stock (see p.14)
1 tsp dried basil
salt and freshly ground black
    pepper, to taste
115g/4oz feta cheese, diced
fresh oregano, to garnish

METHOD

1. Preheat the oven to 220°C/ 400°F/gas mark 6. Lay the tomatoes in a single layer on a baking tray, skin side up, sprinkle with the chopped garlic and drizzle with half the olive oil. Bake in the oven for 30 minutes or until the tomato skins have started to blister. Leave the tomatoes to cool, then remove the skin and discard the seeds.

2. Heat the remaining olive oil in a large saucepan and cook the onion and beetroot until the onion has softened but not browned. Add the tomatoes, stock and dried basil to the pan and bring to the boil. Reduce the heat and simmer for 15–20 minutes, or until the beetroot is tender.

3. Allow the soup to cool a little before pouring into a blender. Process until the mixture is smooth and creamy.

4. Return the soup to a clean pan, season to taste with salt and pepper and heat thoroughly before serving.

5. Serve in warmed bowls garnished with feta cheese and fresh oregano.

WATERCRESS SOUP

This soup has a fresh flavour and vibrant colour. It is an ideal starter because it is light and won't spoil the appetite for the main course.

INGREDIENTS *Serves 4*

60g/2oz butter

1 small onion, finely chopped

60g/2oz plain flour

1 litre/1¾ pints warm vegetable stock (see p.14)

350g/12oz young watercress, coarsely chopped

450ml/15fl oz single cream

1 tsp freshly squeezed lemon juice

salt and freshly ground black pepper, to taste

METHOD

1. Melt the butter in a large saucepan over a medium heat and sauté the onion until it is soft and translucent.

2. Add the flour and cook, stirring constantly, for 2 minutes.

3. Remove the pan from the heat and then gradually whisk in the warm vegetable stock, making sure there are no lumps forming. Once all the stock is incorporated, return the pan to the heat and bring the liquid to a gentle simmer.

4. Add the watercress, cover, and cook over a low heat for 20 minutes.

5. Pureé the soup in batches in a blender until it is smooth and creamy.

6. Pour the soup into a clean saucepan, stir in the single cream and lemon juice and season to taste with salt and pepper. Heat gently before serving.

VARIATION

Replace half the watercress with fresh garden peas and follow the recipe as before.

PART 3

HEARTY SOUPS

The definition of a hearty soup is one that is full of chunky meat or vegetables. It is often served with dumplings, making it a satisfying and comforting meal on a cold winter's evening.

MAKING HEARTY SOUPS

—••••●●••—

Curl up in front of the fire with a rug over your knees and tuck into one of these comforting soups. From cosy staples such as roasted pumpkin to more unusual ones infused with ginger and spices, they are mouth-watering and full of goodness.

The soups in this section are filling and designed to be a one-pot meal when accompanied by light, fluffy dumplings or served with some lovely crusty bread. They will satisfy even the heartiest appetite and, like cream soups, rely on a good stock.

Many of these recipes include pasta, rice, beans or root vegetables. The main difference from the earlier section is that these soups are not entirely puréed at the end of the cooking time – most of the ingredients are left chunky.

Hearty soups can be as straightforward or as adventurous as you want; there is no limit to the ingredients you can use. Once you have tried a few of the recipes here, there is no reason why you should not experiment with flavours of your own. In fact anything goes when making soup, as it is very difficult to produce a bad one. Next time you cook a hearty soup, make double the quantity and put some in the freezer. That way you will have a ready-made dinner when you are too busy to cook.

As before, the amount of salt and pepper used is up to you, but no seasoning should be added until the end of the cooking time. It is lovely to have a variety of fresh herbs to hand for using in soups, but if you have a good supply of dried ones these will suffice – remember to halve the quantity given for fresh herbs.

ASPARAGUS & MUSHROOM SOUP

The combination of asparagus, dried mushrooms and wild rice
gives this soup a hearty flavour.

INGREDIENTS *Serves 4*

175g/6oz mixture of long grain
  and wild rice, cooked
115g/4oz dried mushrooms
  (mixture of porcini, shiitake
  and straw)
250ml/8fl oz boiling water
1 tbsp olive oil
1 red onion, chopped
2 garlic cloves, crushed
450g/1lb asparagus, cut into
  1cm/½in pieces
1 tsp dried thyme
750ml/1¼ pints hot vegetable
  stock (see p.14)
2 tbsp cornflour
175g/6oz can evaporated milk
salt and freshly ground black
  pepper, to taste
1 tsp lemon juice

METHOD

1. Cook the rice according to the
instructions on the packet, drain
and set to one side.

2. Soak the mushrooms in the
boiling water for 20 minutes,
then drain and chop, reserving
the water.

3. Heat the oil in a large
saucepan over a medium heat,
add the onion and garlic and
sauté for 2 minutes. Add the
asparagus and sauté for a further
3 minutes.

4. Add the mushrooms, rice and
thyme and stir to combine. Add
the reserved mushroom water
and stock and bring to the boil.

5. Whisk the cornflour into the
evaporated milk and pour into
the pan, stirring. Bring back to
the boil and cook for 5 minutes or
until the soup has thickened.

6. Remove from the heat, season
with salt and pepper and add
the lemon juice. Give the soup a
good stir and serve while still hot.

BEAN SOUP

This is a filling soup that can easily act as a main course with some chunks of bread and cheese.

INGREDIENTS *Serves 6*

2 tbsp olive oil

2 onions, chopped

2 garlic cloves, crushed

200g/7oz pancetta, chopped

2 carrots, chopped

2 celery sticks, chopped

2 × 400g/14oz cans chopped tomatoes

375g/13oz savoy cabbage, shredded

1 courgette, chopped

2 sprigs of fresh thyme

2 litres/3½ pints hot beef stock (see p.13)

400g/14oz can borlotti beans, rinsed and drained

salt and freshly ground black pepper, to taste

TO SERVE:

6 thick slices of ciabatta bread

3 garlic cloves, halved

extra virgin olive oil

METHOD

1. Heat the oil in a large saucepan over a medium heat. Add the onion, garlic and pancetta and cook for about 5 minutes, stirring, until the onion has softened.

2. Add the carrot, celery, tomatoes, cabbage, courgette, thyme and hot stock. Bring to the boil, then reduce the heat and cook, uncovered, for 30 minutes to allow the flavours to infuse.

3. Add the borlotti beans and continue to simmer for a further 20 minutes, uncovered. Season to taste with salt and freshly ground pepper and serve in individual bowls.

4. Lightly toast the ciabatta bread on both sides, then rub the surface of one side with the cut garlic cloves. Drizzle the bread with olive oil.

BEEF & BARLEY SOUP

Almost a stew, this meaty soup makes a wonderful lunch on a crisp winter's day.

INGREDIENTS *Serves 6*
900g/2lb chuck steak
1 tbsp olive oil
2 onions, finely chopped
2 garlic cloves, crushed
½ small white cabbage, shredded
2 carrots, chopped
2 celery sticks, chopped
2 bay leaves
150g/5½oz pearl barley
500ml/16fl oz beef stock (see p.13)
1 tbsp tomato purée
1 litre/1¾ pints water
salt and freshly ground black pepper, to taste
2 tbsp chopped fresh parsley

METHOD
1. Trim the fat from the chuck steak, then cut the meat into 1cm/½in pieces.
2. Heat the oil in a large saucepan over medium heat and add the onion and garlic. Cook for about 5–6 minutes or until the onion is softened and just starting to go brown.
3. Add the beef and cook for a further 3 minutes or until it is browned on all sides.
4. Add the remaining ingredients, except the salt and pepper and chopped parsley, and bring to the boil. Reduce the heat, and simmer, covered, for about 3 hours, stirring occasionally.
5. At the end of the cooking time season with salt and pepper and stir in the chopped parsley.

BROCCOLI & CHICKEN SOUP

A lovely chunky soup that can be made using up leftover chicken pieces from the Sunday roast.

INGREDIENTS *Serves 4*

2 boneless chicken breasts (or
   leftover cooked chicken)
1 tbsp olive oil
1 onion, chopped
1 garlic clove, finely chopped
2 celery sticks, chopped
1 large potato, peeled and diced
600ml/1 pint hot chicken stock
   (see p.12)
350g/12oz broccoli florets
2 tsp cornflour
salt and freshly ground black
   pepper, to taste

METHOD

1. If you are using uncooked chicken, remove the skin and cut the meat into 2cm/¾in pieces. Heat the oil in a large saucepan and cook the chicken pieces until almost done. Remove the chicken from the pan and set to one side. If the chicken is already cooked, simply cut it up in the same fashion.

2. Sauté the onion for 5 minutes in the oil, then add the garlic, celery and potato and cook for a further 3 minutes.

3. Add the hot stock and half the broccoli to the pan and bring to the boil. Cover, reduce the heat and simmer for about 15 minutes until the vegetables are tender. Pour into a blender and process until smooth.

4. Pour the soup into a clean saucepan and add the remaining broccoli and the chicken pieces. Cover and cook for about 6 minutes or until the broccoli is just tender.

5. Mix the cornflour with a little water and add to the pan. Continue to cook, stirring, until the soup has thickened. Season and serve piping hot.

BUTTERBEAN & CARROT SOUP

The lovely texture of the butterbeans complements the sweet carrot in this soup, which is not only nutritious but very filling, too.

INGREDIENTS *Serves 4*

30g/1oz unsalted butter

1 large onion, chopped

2 garlic cloves, finely chopped

6 carrots, diced

2 medium-sized potatoes, peeled and diced

500ml/16fl oz hot vegetable stock (see p.14)

1 tbsp chopped parsley, plus extra for garnish

½ tsp cayenne pepper

½ tsp mustard seeds

200g/7oz can butter beans, drained

2 tbsp tomato purée

salt and freshly ground black pepper, to taste

METHOD

1. Melt the butter in a large saucepan over a medium heat and sauté the onion for 5 minutes or until softened.

2. Add the garlic, carrots and potatoes and cook for a further 3 minutes, stirring occasionally.

3. Add the hot stock, tablespoon of chopped parsley, cayenne pepper and mustard seeds to the pan and bring to the boil. Turn down the heat, cover and simmer for 15 minutes or until the potatoes and carrots are cooked through.

4. Remove the pan from the heat and allow the soup to cool slightly. Purée approximately one-third of the soup in a blender, then return it to the pan with the remainder of the vegetables. Add the butter beans and tomato purée and mix well.

5. Reheat the soup, season to taste with salt and black pepper and serve immediately, garnished with a scattering of chopped parsley.

CABBAGE, HAM & BACON SOUP

This soup only takes about 20 minutes to prepare, but makes a filling and satisfying meal served with some fresh bread.

INGREDIENTS *Serves 4*

1 tbsp olive oil

1 onion, finely chopped

1 carrot, chopped

1 celery stick, chopped

2 garlic cloves, finely chopped

500g/1lb 2oz floury potatoes, peeled and chopped

1 litre/1¾ pints hot chicken stock (see p.12)

8 rashers streaky bacon

175g/6oz cooked gammon, cut into 1cm/½in cubes

225g/8oz savoy cabbage, shredded

salt and freshly ground black pepper, to taste

METHOD

1. Heat the oil in a large saucepan over a medium heat and add the onion. Sauté until softened and then add the carrot, celery, garlic and potatoes. Cook, covered, for a further 5 minutes, or until the vegetables start to soften.

2. Add the stock and bring the mixture to a boil. Simmer for 5 minutes or until all the vegetables are tender.

3. While the vegetables are cooking, grill or fry the bacon until it is crisp and then cut into thin strips. Set to one side.

4. Let the soup cool a little, then pour into a blender and process until smooth. Return the soup to a clean pan.

5. Add the gammon and shredded cabbage and simmer for a few minutes until the gammon is heated through and the cabbage is tender. Season to taste with salt and pepper.

6. Serve immediately in individual bowls, garnished with the crispy bacon.

CHICKEN AND PASTA SOUP

This recipe has been a favourite with students for many years because it is filling, yet cheap and simple to make.

INGREDIENTS *Serves 4*

2 tbsp olive oil

1 onion, finely chopped

1 celery stick, finely chopped

2 garlic cloves, finely chopped

1 carrot, finely chopped

1 potato, peeled and finely chopped

1 tsp dried thyme

1.5 litres/2¾ pints hot chicken stock (see p.12)

200g/7oz tiny pasta shapes, such as orzo

125g/4½oz kale, finely shredded

200g/7oz cooked chicken, cut into strips

salt and freshly ground black pepper, to taste

Parmesan shavings, to garnish

METHOD

1. Heat the oil in a large saucepan over a medium heat and add the onion. Sauté until softened, then add the celery, garlic, carrot, potato and dried thyme. Cook for a further 3–4 minutes until the vegetables have softened but are not browned.

2. Add the stock and pasta, cover, and simmer for 8 minutes, or until the pasta is cooked.

3. Stir the kale and chicken into the soup, check the seasoning and simmer for another 5 minutes or until the chicken is heated through and the kale has wilted.

4. Serve immediately in individual bowls and garnish with shavings of Parmesan.

CHICKPEA & PEPPER SOUP

This soup is a typical Spanish recipe which is served
with fresh bread and a side salad of hard-boiled eggs,
onions and cucumber chunks.

INGREDIENTS *Serves 4*

4 whole garlic cloves
450g/1lb canned chickpeas,
    drained
1 litre/1¾ pints vegetable stock
    (see p.14)
4 tbsp olive oil
3 rashers unsmoked bacon, diced
2 bay leaves
½ tsp coriander seeds
1 onion, roughly chopped
4 tbsp chopped fresh parsley,
    plus extra to garnish
2 tbsp fresh mint, chopped
1 tsp dried oregano
1 large potato, peeled and cut
    into chunks
1 red pepper, deseeded and cut
    into strips
large handful of spinach,
    shredded
salt and freshly ground black
    pepper, to taste

METHOD

1. Place the garlic cloves under
a hot grill and cook until their
papery skins have started
to char.

2. Put the chickpeas in a large
saucepan with the stock,
2 tablespoons of olive oil,
bacon, bay leaves, coriander
seeds, onion and herbs and
bring to the boil. Reduce the
heat and simmer gently for 30
minutes or until the onion is soft.

3. Add the potato and continue to
simmer until it is tender.

4. While the potato is cooking,
heat the remaining olive oil in a
frying pan and fry the strips of
red pepper and the garlic cloves
squeezed out of their papery
skins. Cook until the peppers
have softened and started to
caramelize, then set to one side.

5. Remove the bay leaves from the soup. Stir in the spinach and bring the soup back to the boil. Season with salt and pepper to taste.

6. Ladle the soup into individual bowls with a spoonful of the peppers and their garlic-flavoured oil over the top. Sprinkle with parsley and serve with plenty of fresh bread.

PAN CON TOMATE

Traditionally this soup is served with 'pan con tomate', a rustic bread that has been rubbed with tomato and garlic. It is very easy to make and really adds authenticity to the meal.

INGREDIENTS *Makes 8 slices*

8 slices sourdough or rustic
    country bread, cut into
    2cm¾in slices
4 garlic cloves, cut in half
4 small vine-ripe tomatoes, cut
    in half
2 tbsp extra virgin olive oil
1 tsp coarse sea salt
1 tsp freshly ground peppercorns

VARIATION

If you want to use dried chickpeas, place 225g/8oz in sufficient water to cover them and leave to soak overnight. Increase the cooking time in Step 2 to 1½–2 hours or until chickpeas are soft.

Grill the bread for about 2–3 minutes on each side or until it is lightly browned. Using a fresh half clove of garlic for each slice, rub the cut side of the clove over one side of the bread while it is still warm. Rub the cut tomato over the bread, pressing firmly so that the pulp penetrates the surface. Drizzle olive oil over the bread and sprinkle with salt and pepper. Serve warm.

CLAM CHOWDER

This is a traditional recipe for clam chowder, New England style, which means it has a rich, creamy base and plenty of clams.

INGREDIENTS *Serves 4*

2 rashers smoked streaky
   bacon, diced
1 small onion, chopped
450g/1lb russet potatoes, peeled
   and diced
1 tbsp plain flour
2 × 280g/10oz cans clams,
   drained, reserving the liquid
250ml/8fl oz whole milk
250ml/8fl oz double cream
salt and freshly ground black
   pepper, to taste

METHOD

1. Heat a large saucepan over
a medium heat and dry fry the
bacon until it is brown and has
released some of its fat. Add the
onion and sauté until translucent
but not browned.
2. Add the diced potato and stir
until it has been coated in the
bacon fat. Add the flour and

sauté, stirring, until the onion and
potatoes are golden.
3. Pour in the reserved clam juice
and bring to the boil. Reduce the
heat and simmer, covered, for
20 minutes or until the potato is
tender but not broken up.
4. Once the potato is cooked, stir
in the drained clams, milk and
cream and season to taste with
salt and pepper. Stir and heat
through, but do not allow to boil.
Serve immediately.

CHEF'S TIP

Clam chowder is extra-
special if you can get hold
of fresh clams. Clean,
shuck and steam the clams,
remembering to reserve the
cooking liquid.

COURGETTE, POTATO & PEA SOUP

If you grow your own vegetables you will probably find that you have a lot of courgettes ready for picking at the same time. This chunky soup is a great way to use them up and it can be frozen, too.

INGREDIENTS *Serves 2*

30g/1oz unsalted butter
1 small onion, finely chopped
1 garlic clove, crushed
150g/5½oz potato, peeled
    and diced
225g/8oz courgettes, cut
    into chunks
2 tsp chopped fresh coriander
600ml/1 pint hot vegetable stock
    (see p.14)
2 tbsp light soy sauce
150g/5½oz fresh or frozen peas
salt and freshly ground black
    pepper, to taste

TO GARNISH:
60g/2oz Parmesan cheese, grated
1 tbsp chopped fresh coriander

METHOD

1. Heat the butter in a large saucepan over a medium heat. Add the onion and garlic and cook for about 5 minutes or until the onion has softened but not browned.

2. Add the potato, courgettes and coriander and cook for a further 2–3 minutes.

3. Add the stock and soy sauce and bring to the boil. Reduce the heat and simmer for 15 minutes or until the potatoes are cooked but not broken up.

4. Add the peas and cook for a further 2 minutes.

5. Season with salt and black pepper and spoon into individual bowls. Serve with freshly grated Parmesan cheese and coriander sprinkled over the surface.

If you like a richer flavour, you can add a tablespoon of green pesto to the stock.

CURRY NOODLE SOUP

This soup has a lot of ingredients to assemble, but the wonderful blend of spices and heat makes it an irresistible winter warmer.

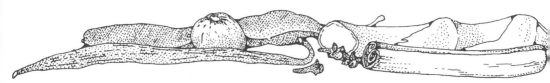

INGREDIENTS *Serves 4*

2 tbsp olive oil

2 shallots, finely chopped

3 garlic cloves, finely chopped

1 tbsp minced lemongrass

2.5cm/1in fresh root ginger, peeled and grated

1 tbsp yellow Thai curry paste

1 tbsp curry powder

1 tsp hot chilli powder

2 × 400g/14oz cans coconut milk

1 litre/1¾ pints chicken stock (see p.12)

2 tbsp fish sauce

2 tsp sugar

300g/10oz sugarsnap peas

1 sweet potato, peeled and diced

450g/1lb dried vermicelli rice noodles

350g/12oz cooked chicken breast, skinned and cut into matchsticks

2 spring onions, thinly sliced

3 red jalapeño chillies, thinly sliced, with seeds

1 tbsp chopped fresh coriander

1 lime, cut into wedges, to serve

METHOD

1. Heat the oil in a large saucepan over a medium heat and add the shallots, garlic, lemongrass and ginger. Cook for 1 minute, stirring, then reduce the heat to low and stir in the curry paste, curry powder and chilli powder. Shake the cans of coconut milk and add one canful to the pan, stirring, until thick and fragrant – about 2 minutes.

2. Add the remaining coconut milk, stock, fish sauce and sugar and bring to the boil. Reduce the heat, cover and simmer on a very low heat while you prepare the other ingredients.

3. Cook the sugarsnap peas in a little lightly salted boiling water for about 30 seconds. Remove with a slotted spoon, drain and rinse in cold water to keep their colour. Set aside.

4. Cook the sweet potato in the same water for 7 minutes, then remove with a slotted spoon and rinse under cold water. Set to one side.

5. Bring the same water back to the boil, add the vermicelli and cook until *al dente* – this should take about 6 minutes. Drain and set aside.

6. Add the chicken to the stock in the saucepan and simmer for 10 minutes or until the chicken has been heated through. Add the sweet potato, stir and cook for a further minute.

7. Heat the vermicelli and sugarsnap peas in the microwave for about 1 minute, or until heated through, then divide evenly between the individual bowls.

8. Pour the hot soup over the noodles, then scatter the spring onions, chopped chillies and coriander over the soup. Serve with lime wedges on the side.

- - - - - - - - - - - - - - - - -

VARIATION

You can add different vegetables to this soup and still retain the Asian flavours. Try pak choi, Thai asparagus, baby sweetcorn or fresh shiitake mushrooms.

- - - - - - - - - - - - - - - - -

LAMB & BEAN SOUP

The lamb absorbs all the flavours and simply melts in your mouth in this filling and hearty soup.

INGREDIENTS *Serves 8*

200g/7oz dried cannellini beans
2 tbsp olive oil
3 lamb shanks (a total weight of approx. 750g/1lb 10oz)
2 onions, finely chopped
1 garlic clove, finely chopped
1 red chilli, deseeded and finely chopped
2 carrots, peeled and diced
2 celery sticks, finely chopped
500ml/16fl oz chicken stock (see p.12)
600ml/1pt water
400g/14oz can chopped tomatoes
1 tbsp fresh dill, finely chopped
2 tbsp lemon juice
salt and freshly ground black pepper, to taste

METHOD

1. Soak the butter beans in cold water overnight.

2. Heat the olive oil in a large saucepan. Add the lamb shanks and fry rapidly on a fairly high heat until they are browned on all sides. Remove the lamb from the pan and set to one side.

3. Add the onion, garlic, chilli, carrots and celery to the oil in the pan and cook over a medium heat until softened, stirring occasionally.

4. Return the lamb to the pan with the drained beans, chicken stock and water. Bring to the boil, then reduce the heat and simmer, covered, for 1 hour.

5. Remove the lamb and when cool enough to handle shred the meat from the bones and return it to the pan. Add the tomatoes and simmer for a further hour.

6. Just before serving, stir in the chopped dill and lemon juice and season to taste.

LOBSTER BISQUE

With its luscious chunks of lobster, this luxurious soup can be eaten as a main course.

INGREDIENTS *Serves 4*

120g/4¼oz unsalted butter
500g/1lb 2oz lobster meat, cut into chunks (shells reserved)
1 onion, finely chopped
1 large potato, peeled and cut into 2cm/¾in chunks
1 large carrot, chopped
1 celery stick, finely chopped
1 garlic clove, finely chopped
2 tbsp plain flour
4 tbsp dry sherry
250ml/8fl oz fish stock (see p.15)
1 tbsp tomato purée
2 bay leaves
1 sprig of thyme
½ tsp sweet paprika
500ml/16fl oz double cream
salt and freshly ground black pepper, to taste
1 tbsp chopped fresh parsley

METHOD

1. Melt the butter in a large saucepan and add the lobster shells, broken into pieces. Reduce the heat and fry for 2 minutes, stirring. Add the vegetables, sprinkle in the flour and cook for 2–3 minutes. Remove the shells and deglaze the pan by adding the sherry, letting it boil for a minute and scraping up any sediment as you do so.

2. Add the stock, tomato purée, bay leaves, thyme and paprika, then bring to the boil. Cover, reduce the heat and simmer for 20 minutes.

3. Strain the soup through a fine sieve, pressing the vegetables with the back of a spoon.

4. Pour the soup back into a clean saucepan, add the cream and season to taste. Add the lobster and cook on medium until it is heated through. Serve garnished with fresh parsley.

MEDITERRANEAN FISH SOUP

The list of ingredients may look daunting, but once you have got them all together the making of this fragrant soup is very simple and will fill your kitchen with a wonderful aroma.

INGREDIENTS *Serves 8*
90ml/3fl oz olive oil
4 onions, chopped
115g/4oz fennel bulb, chopped
115g/4oz leek, white parts only, chopped
2 celery sticks, chopped
2 carrots, chopped
4 garlic cloves, finely chopped
300ml/10fl oz dry white wine
2 star anise
400g/14oz can chopped tomatoes
140g/5oz tomato purée
good pinch of saffron strands
3 strips of orange zest
1 tsp mixed Italian herbs

900g/2lb mixed fish (such as cod, haddock, salmon) filleted and cut into 2.5cm/1in chunks
115g/4oz large prawns, shelled
115g/4oz fresh white crab meat
3.5 litres/6 pints hot fish stock (see p.15)
½ tsp cayenne pepper
salt and freshly ground black pepper, to taste

TO GARNISH:
6 slices baguette
1 tbsp extra virgin olive oil
60g/2oz Parmesan cheese, grated

METHOD

1. Heat the olive oil in a large saucepan and add the chopped onions, fennel, leek, celery, carrots and garlic. Sweat the vegetables over a medium heat until they start to soften, but do not brown. Remove the vegetables from the pan and set aside.

2. Deglaze the saucepan by adding the wine and star anise and allowing the mixture to boil for a few minutes. Make sure you scrape the bottom of the pan to loosen all the tasty sediment.

3. Return the vegetables to the pan and add the remaining ingredients with the exception of the cayenne pepper, salt and black pepper. Bring the mixture to a boil, then reduce the heat and simmer for 30 minutes, uncovered.

4. Ladle one-third of the soup into a blender and process until smooth. This will help to intensify the flavour of the stock. Return the purée to the soup, season with cayenne pepper, salt and ground black pepper and reheat before serving.

5. Cut the baguette into 2cm/¾in slices and toast on one side until golden brown. Drizzle the uncooked side of the bread with olive oil and sprinkle generously with grated Parmesan cheese.

6. Spoon the soup into separate bowls and float the Parmesan bread on the surface, toasted side down, so that it absorbs the liquid from the fish soup.

- - - - - - - - - - - - - - - - - -

VARIATIONS

- Try using a different combination of fish and seafood, such as gurnard, red mullet, monkfish, squid and mussels.

- Add 175g/6oz small new potatoes, cut into small dice, along with the other vegetables.

- - - - - - - - - - - - - - - - - -

MINESTRONE WITH POTATO DUMPLINGS

This is probably the best-known of all the hearty soups. To make it more of a meal, it is served here with potato dumplings delicately flavoured with snipped chives and parsley.

INGREDIENTS *Serves 4*

2 tbsp olive oil

1 onion, chopped

250g/9oz carrots, diced

3 celery sticks, sliced

1 head of broccoli, broken into florets

2 garlic cloves, finely chopped

2 tomatoes, skinned, deseeded and chopped

175g/6oz savoy cabbage, shredded

2 sprigs of fresh rosemary

1.5 litres/2¾ pints hot vegetable stock (see p.14)

60g/2oz frozen peas

salt and freshly ground black pepper, to taste

3 tbsp grated Parmesan cheese, to garnish

FOR THE DUMPLINGS:

4 baking potatoes

30g/1oz fresh breadcrumbs

1 egg

2 tbsp milk

1 tbsp flour, plus extra for rolling

½ tsp salt

¼ tsp ground white pepper

3 tbsp snipped chives

1 tbsp chopped fresh parsley

METHOD

1. To make the minestrone, heat the oil in a large saucepan over a medium heat and sauté the onion, carrots, celery, broccoli and garlic for 5 minutes.

2. Add the tomatoes, cabbage and fresh rosemary and stir to combine.

3. Add the stock and bring to the boil. Turn down the heat, cover and simmer for 15 minutes, or until the vegetables are just soft. Add the peas and cook for another 5 minutes.

4. To make the potato dumplings, scrub the potatoes and put them in lightly salted boiling water without peeling them. Cover and cook until they are soft.

5. Allow the potatoes to cool, then remove the flesh from the skins and pass it through a potato ricer.

6. In a medium-sized bowl, combine the breadcrumbs, egg, milk, flour, salt, pepper, chives and parsley. Add the riced potato and mix well to combine. If you find the ingredients are too dry,

add another egg. The mixture should be soft, but needs to retain its shape when moulded.

7. Lightly flour your hands and mould the dumpling mixture into small walnut-sized balls, then roll them in flour.

8. Drop the dumplings into the hot soup and cook for 15 minutes, covered, until cooked through. Season to taste and serve the soup in individual bowls with a few dumplings in each one and a garnish of some grated Parmesan cheese.

VARIATION – SUET DUMPLINGS

115g/4oz self-raising flour
60g/2oz shredded suet
salt and black pepper

Mix to a dough with cold water, roll into balls and cook in the hot soup for 15–20 minutes.

MIXED VEGETABLE SOUP

This soup is packed with vegetables and has a lovely delicate, warming flavour.

INGREDIENTS *Serves 4*
30g/1oz unsalted butter
1 small onion, chopped
1 small leek, thinly sliced
1 large carrot, diced
1 fennel bulb, sliced
225g/8oz swede, cut into cubes
225g/8oz potato, peeled and cut
  into cubes
several sprigs of fresh thyme
1 bay leaf
several sprigs of fresh parsley
600ml/1 pint hot vegetable stock
  (see p.14)
400g/14oz can chopped
  tomatoes
salt and freshly ground black
  pepper, to taste
snipped chives, to garnish

METHOD
1. Melt the butter in a large saucepan over a medium heat and add the onion. Cook for about 5 minutes, stirring occasionally, until it has softened but not browned.

2. Add the leek, carrot, fennel, swede and potato and cook for a further 5 minutes, or until the vegetables have started to soften a little.

3. Make a bouquet garni out of the thyme, bay leaf and parsley and tie securely. Add to the pan together with the stock and tomatoes. Bring to the boil, cover, then reduce the heat to a simmer. Cook for 45 minutes or until the vegetables are tender.

4. Remove the bouquet garni and season to taste with salt and pepper. Serve in individual bowls, garnished with chives and with large wedges of granary or wholemeal bread for dunking.

MULLIGATAWNY

Mulligatawny is a spicy soup that gets its name from the Tamil words meaning 'pepper' and 'water'. It is up to you just how spicy you make it.

INGREDIENTS *Serves 4–6*

60g/2oz unsalted butter

1 onion, chopped

2 celery sticks, chopped

1 carrot, diced

1 potato, peeled and diced

1 parsnip, diced

1 tbsp plain flour

2 tbsp curry powder

1 litre/1¾ pints vegetable stock
  (see p.14)

4 tbsp basmati rice

½ eating apple, peeled, cored
  and diced

1 tsp dried thyme

100ml/3½fl oz double cream

salt and freshly ground black
  pepper, to taste

METHOD

1. Melt the butter in a large saucepan over a medium heat and add the onion, celery, carrot, potato and parsnip. Sauté for 5–6 minutes until they are softened and starting to brown.

2. Add the flour and curry powder and cook for 5 more minutes, stirring so that all the ingredients are mixed.

3. Add the stock, bring to the boil, then reduce the heat, cover, and simmer for 30 minutes.

4. Add the rice, apple and thyme and simmer for a further 20 minutes or so, until the rice is cooked.

5. Stir in the cream, season with salt and pepper and reheat the soup gently without allowing it to boil.

6. Serve in bowls garnished with thinly sliced red chillies, chopped tomato and some lightly toasted desiccated coconut.

PUMPKIN MINESTRONE

This variation of minestrone is chunky – in fact it is so thick you could probably stand your spoon up in it!

INGREDIENTS *Serves 4*

2 tbsp olive oil

1 large leek, finely sliced

1 celery stick, finely sliced

1 large carrot, diced

3 tomatoes, skinned and diced

1.2 litre/2 pints hot vegetable stock (see p.14)

225g/8oz pumpkin flesh, diced

1 large potato, peeled and diced

bouquet garni, made up of thyme, parsley, basil and a bay leaf

60g/2oz quick-cook macaroni

salt and black pepper, to taste

1 tbsp pesto

METHOD

1. Heat the oil in a large pan and add the leek, celery and carrot. Cook for about 10 minutes until softened, but not browned.

2. Add the tomatoes, stock, pumpkin, potato and bouquet garni and bring to the boil. Turn down the heat and simmer for about 20 minutes, covered, or until the vegetables are tender.

3. Stir in the pasta and cook for another 15 minutes. Remove the bouquet garni and season to taste. Add the pesto. Serve with rustic bread and a little grated Parmesan cheese.

PESTO

Process 6 garlic cloves, a handful of basil leaves, 60g/2oz pine nuts, 60g/2oz pecorino cheese, 1 tsp salt and 60ml/2fl oz olive oil in a blender. When it is a smooth paste, trickle in extra olive oil with the motor running, until you have a thick sauce.

SAUSAGE, LEEK & LENTIL SOUP

A comforting and spicy soup ideal for a cold day, this is packed with protein and vegetable goodness.

INGREDIENTS *Serves 4*

1 tbsp olive oil
1 large onion, chopped
2 carrots, diced
300g/10oz potatoes, peeled
　and diced
1 leek, thinly sliced
2 garlic cloves, crushed
300g/10oz hot Italian sausage
1.5 litres/2¾ pints beef stock
　(see p.13)
200g/7oz red lentils
½ tsp crushed red pepper flakes
½ tsp dried oregano
½ tsp dried thyme
½ tsp fennel seeds
1 bay leaf
salt and freshly ground black
　pepper, to taste
1 tbsp chopped fresh parsley

METHOD

1. Heat the oil in a large frying pan over a medium heat and add the onion, carrots, potatoes, leek and garlic. Sauté until they are starting to soften. Transfer the vegetables to a large saucepan.

2. Skin and slice the sausage, then fry the slices in the frying pan until browned on both sides. Transfer to the saucepan.

3. Pour the stock over the sausage and vegetables, add the lentils and season with the red pepper flakes, oregano, thyme, fennel seeds and bay leaf. Bring to boiling point, then turn down the heat and simmer for 30–40 minutes, or until the lentils are tender.

4. Remove the bay leaf, pour one-third of the soup into a blender and process until smooth. Return the purée to the pan, season the soup with salt and pepper and serve garnished with chopped parsley.

SCOTCH BROTH

A filling, hearty soup that originated in Scotland, this can be made with either lamb or beef.

INGREDIENTS *Serves 8*

60g/2oz split peas, soaked overnight and drained

60g/2oz barley, soaked overnight and drained

1 lamb neck fillet, trimmed of fat and diced

1 litre/1¾ pints vegetable stock (see p.14)

1 litre/1¾ pints water

1 onion, chopped

1 leek, chopped

2 small turnips, diced

2 carrots, diced

½ savoy cabbage, shredded

salt and freshly ground black pepper, to taste

1 tbsp chopped fresh parsley

METHOD

1. In a large saucepan, combine the split peas, barley, lamb, stock and water and bring to the boil. With a slotted spoon, skim off any scum that rises to the surface.

2. After 10 minutes, add the onion, leek, turnips and carrots and bring back to the boil. Reduce the heat, cover, and simmer gently for 3 hours.

3. Add the shredded cabbage, cover and simmer for a further hour.

4. Before serving, taste the broth and season to taste. Add the chopped parsley and serve in individual bowls.

CHEF'S TIP

Scotch broth was originally made from mutton, which you can still buy from a butcher. Use any vegetables that are in season.

SPICY PEA & VEGETABLE SOUP

This is pea soup with a difference – adding a little spice makes it something really special. Adjust the amount of chillies to taste.

INGREDIENTS *Serves 4*

100g/3½oz dried brown peas, soaked overnight
1 tbsp olive oil
1 tsp cumin seeds
1 onion, sliced
3 garlic cloves, finely chopped
4 rashers smoked streaky bacon, diced
2.5cm/1in fresh root ginger, grated
2 tsp garam masala
2 green chillies, deseeded and finely chopped
400g/14oz cauliflower, broken into small florets
400g/14oz pumpkin flesh, diced
750ml/1¼ pints hot vegetable stock (see p.14)
1 tsp tomato purée
salt and freshly ground black pepper, to taste
soured cream and chopped fresh parsley, to garnish

METHOD

1. Drain and rinse the peas and set aside.

2. Heat the olive oil in a large saucepan over a medium heat and sauté the cumin seeds, onion, garlic, bacon, ginger, garam masala and chillies for about 2 minutes.

3. Add the cauliflower and pumpkin, sauté for a further 2 minutes then add the stock, tomato purée and soaked peas. Stir to combine, bring to the boil, then reduce the heat and simmer for 30–35 minutes or until the vegetables are soft.

4. Season the soup to taste with salt and black pepper and then spoon into individual bowls while steaming hot. Garnish each one with a little soured cream and chopped parsley to finish.

SMOKED HADDOCK CHOWDER

This creamy, filling chowder is made with smoked haddock
and is not dissimilar to the Scottish cullen skink.

INGREDIENTS *Serves 4*
600ml/1 pint whole milk
1 small bunch of flat-leaf parsley,
    finely chopped, stalks reserved
1 bay leaf
350g/12oz undyed smoked
    haddock fillet
60g/2oz unsalted butter
1 onion, chopped
1 leek, white parts only, finely
    sliced
1 carrot, diced
2 tbsp plain flour
85g/3oz baby spinach leaves,
    finely shredded

1 tsp dried dill
198g/7oz can sweetcorn, drained
175ml/6fl oz double cream
salt and freshly ground black
    pepper, to taste

METHOD
1. Pour the milk into a large
saucepan and add the parsley
stalks along with the bay leaf
and haddock. Bring the milk to
a gentle boil and cook for
3 minutes. Remove the pan from
the heat and leave the flavours
to infuse for 10 minutes.

2. Lift the haddock out of the milk, using a slotted spoon, and set aside. Strain the milk through a fine sieve and set aside.

3. Melt the butter in a large saucepan, add the onion, leek and carrot and cook gently for about 10 minutes or until the vegetables are starting to soften, but do not let them brown.

4. Stir the flour into the vegetable mixture and cook for 2 minutes, stirring continuously to make sure that the mixture does not stick to the bottom of the pan.

5. Slowly add the strained milk to the saucepan and mix it in thoroughly. Cook over a gentle heat, stirring continuously, until the mixture has thickened.

6. Flake the smoked haddock into the soup, leaving it in fairly large chunks but making sure that you remove any bones that are present.

7. Add the spinach, dill, sweetcorn, cream and chopped parsley leaves to the soup, stirring gently, taking care not to break up the fish too much. Heat gently and simmer for a further 5 minutes, making sure you do not allow it to boil.

8. Season the soup to taste with salt and black pepper and serve immediately with crusty bread.

VARIATIONS

- If you want an even more filling soup, serve the chowder with a lightly poached egg on top.

- Replace the carrot with 900g/2lb peeled and diced potatoes and increase the cooking time slightly in Step 3 until the potatoes are cooked.

- Replace the smoked haddock with lightly smoked salmon fillets.

VEGETABLE & GAMMON SOUP

This is another hearty soup, with its vegetables, pearl barley
and chunks of gammon.

INGREDIENTS *Serves 4*
60g/2oz smoked streaky
    bacon, diced
1 onion, chopped
100g/3½oz pearl barley
½ tsp freshly grated nutmeg
600ml/1 pint beef stock (see p.13)
200g/7oz precooked smoked
    gammon
225g/8oz pumpkin flesh, diced
1 leek, thinly sliced
2 celery sticks, chopped, leaves
    reserved
salt and freshly ground black
    pepper, to taste

METHOD
1. Dry fry the bacon in a large
saucepan over a medium heat.
Once it has released some of
its fat, add the onion and pearl
barley and sauté for 5 minutes
or until the onion is starting
to soften.

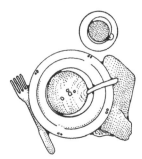

2. Season with nutmeg and add
the beef stock. Bring to the boil,
then reduce the heat to a simmer
and cook, covered, for 20–25
minutes.
3. Cut the gammon into 2.5cm/1in
cubes and add to the saucepan
with the pumpkin, leek and
celery. Bring back to the boil,
then reduce the heat and simmer,
covered, for a further 20–25
minutes or until the vegetables
are soft.
4. Season the soup to taste with
salt and pepper and serve
immediately, garnished with
a few celery leaves.

VENISON SOUP

This is certainly the soup for anyone who enjoys the earthy flavour of game, and although it takes a little longer to cook than most soups it is certainly worth the wait as the meat will melt in your mouth.

INGREDIENTS *Serves 4*

600ml/1 pint water

1.2 litres/2 pints beef stock
  (see p.13)

900g/2lb lean venison, cubed

1 onion, chopped

3 small turnips, peeled and cut
  into chunks

6 small carrots, sliced

2 celery sticks, sliced

200g/7oz pearl barley

2 tsp finely chopped fresh sage

1 tbsp finely chopped fresh
  parsley

90ml/3fl oz red wine (optional)

85g/3oz baby spinach leaves,
  blanched

salt and freshly ground black
  pepper, to taste

METHOD

1. Pour the water and stock into a large saucepan and add the venison. Bring to the boil, then turn down the heat until barely simmering. Cook for 20 minutes, Using a slotted spoon, regularly remove any scum that appears on the surface.

2. Lift out the venison with a slotted spoon and set to one side. Strain the cooking liquid through a fine sieve into a clean saucepan, then add the venison. Cook very slowly, covered, for 2 hours, or until the venison is very tender.

3. Add all the vegetables, barley and herbs, and the wine if you would like an even richer soup. Cover the pan and cook for a further hour or until the barley is tender.

4. Stir in the blanched spinach and season to taste with salt and freshly ground black pepper.

WHITE BEAN & CARROT SOUP

This thick, creamy soup makes a wonderful warming treat, especially if you add a little hot chilli sauce.

INGREDIENTS *Serves 4*
115g/4oz dried haricot beans, soaked overnight and drained
500ml/16fl oz hot vegetable stock (see p.14)
60g/2oz unsalted butter
2 onions, chopped
3 carrots, chopped
1 large potato, peeled and chopped
1 fennel bulb, chopped
3 garlic cloves, crushed
2 tsp finely chopped fresh sage leaves
1 tsp finely chopped fresh rosemary leaves
1 tbsp grated Parmesan cheese
salt and black pepper, to taste

METHOD
1. Put the beans in a large pan with the stock. Bring to the boil, then simmer gently for 1 hour.
2. Melt the butter in a large frying pan. Add the onions, carrots, potato, fennel and garlic and sauté for 5 minutes or until they are starting to soften.
3. Add the vegetables and herbs to the saucepan and bring back to the boil. Reduce the heat and simmer gently for 20 minutes or until the vegetables are tender.
4. Stir in the Parmesan and season to taste before serving.

VARIATIONS

Try adding a teaspoon of hot chilli sauce to the soup or some pieces of skinned and chopped fresh tomato. You could also try using a different type of bean.

PART 4

CLEAR SOUPS

A clear soup or broth is made without any form of thickening agent. It is not puréed to intensify the flavour, but relies instead on herbs and spices and other ingredients to make it taste delicious.

MAKING CLEAR SOUPS

All soups require a good-quality stock as a base, but this is especially the case with a clear soup. Once you have a full-flavoured stock, the remaining ingredients will simply add to the tastiness. As with all soups, be sure to use really fresh produce.

The art of making this type of soup is perhaps the hardest of all to master. The aim when making clear soups is that, regardless of the ingredients added, the final stock must never be cloudy. Very often clear soups contain noodles or pasta of some kind to make them more full-bodied, but the secret of a satisfying clear soup is the infusion of flavours in the broth itself. This may result from simmering meat, poultry, fish, seafood or just vegetables.

As long as you give the stock time to absorb all the flavours, a clear soup can be just as satisfying as a thick or creamy one. Since clear soups do not contain thickening agents like cream or butter, they are generally quite low in calories so are good for people on a diet.

Whether you want to keep your clear soup simple or plan on it acting as the focus for a whole dinner, there are plenty of variations to choose from. The garnish is an important final touch, as it can make the difference between a good, plain meal or an elegant, outstanding dish that any chef would be proud to put on the table.

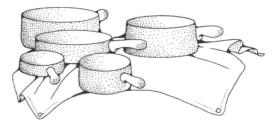

ASPARAGUS & PRAWN SOUP

This delicious soup has an fusion flavour; the rice noodles make it satisfying enough for a main course.

INGREDIENTS *Serves 4*

1 litre/1¾ pints chicken stock
(see p.12)
2 tbsp hoisin sauce
2 tbsp oyster sauce
1 tbsp fish sauce
2cm/¾in fresh root ginger, peeled
and finely sliced
200g/7oz thin rice noodles
100g/3½oz shiitake mushrooms,
sliced
1 green chilli, deseeded and
finely sliced
300g/10oz raw king prawns,
shelled
200g/7oz asparagus spears,
trimmed and cut into
4cm/1½in pieces
100g/3½oz sugarsnap peas,
finely shredded
200g/7oz bean sprouts
salt and freshly ground black
pepper, to taste
fresh coriander, to garnish

METHOD

1. Put the stock, hoisin, oyster and fish sauces and ginger into a large saucepan and bring to the boil. Reduce the heat and simmer gently for 5 minutes.

2. Cook the rice noodles according to the instructions on the packet and set aside.

3. Add the mushrooms and chilli to the stock in the saucepan and boil for 3 minutes. Add the prawns, asparagus and peas and simmer for a further 3–4 minutes or until the prawns are cooked through. Add the bean sprouts and cook for a further minute. Season to taste.

4. Divide the noodles between 4 bowls and pour the soup over the top, making sure the prawns are evenly divided among them. Garnish each bowl with freshly chopped coriander.

BEEF BROTH WITH NOODLES

The basic beef stock is slightly different in this recipe, so you will
need to make a separate batch from the one given on page 13.

INGREDIENTS *Serves 4*

FOR THE STOCK:

2kg/4½lb beef marrow or knuckle
   bones, cut into pieces
2 litres/3½ pints water
1 large onion, chopped
1 large carrot, chopped
½ large daikon radish, chopped
3 spring onions, sliced
5cm/2in fresh root ginger, peeled
   and sliced
1 star anise
2 tbsp rice wine
½ tsp salt

FOR THE SOUP:

1.5 litres/2¾ pints beef stock
   (as above)
2cm/¾in fresh root ginger, peeled
   and finely sliced
3 spring onions, finely sliced
1 sweet red pepper, deseeded
   and thinly sliced

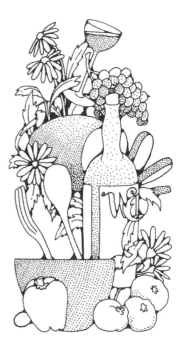

400g/14oz lean beef fillet, thinly
   sliced
400g/14oz white round noodles
salt and freshly ground black
   pepper, to taste
½ tsp sesame oil

METHOD FOR THE STOCK

1. Ask your butcher to chop the beef bones into manageable pieces. Rinse them under cold water, then place them on a large baking tray and bake in a preheated oven at 200°C/400°F/ gas mark 6 for 40–45 minutes.

2. Bring the water to the boil in a large saucepan.

3. Add the beef bones to the pot with the remaining ingredients. Reduce the heat to a simmer, cover, and cook for 1½ hours.

4. Strain the stock through a fine sieve lined with a piece of muslin.

METHOD FOR THE SOUP

1. Put the stock, ginger, 2 spring onions and the pepper into a large saucepan and bring to the boil. Reduce the heat, cover, and simmer for 1 hour.

2. Add the beef to the saucepan and cook for a further 20 minutes.

3. While the soup is cooking, boil the noodles according to the instructions on the packet.

4. Drain the noodles and divide them evenly between 4 bowls. Season the soup to taste then spoon it over the noodles, distributing the beef evenly between the bowls. Dribble a few drops of sesame oil and scatter some slivers of spring onion over each one.

VARIATIONS

Beef broth with noodles can be garnished with a range of different titbits, for example red serrano chillies, deseeded and thinly sliced, thin wedges of lime or sprigs of Asian basil. You can also make a coriander pesto by blending together 2 bunches of coriander leaves with the zest and juice of 1 lemon, 2 garlic cloves and 3 tbsp olive oil. This can be stirred into the soup just before serving to give it an extra kick.

BOUILLABAISSE

There are many different recipes for bouillabaisse – a traditional French fish soup. Here is a really good one.

INGREDIENTS *Serves 6*
1 tbsp olive oil
450g/1lb leeks, thinly sliced
1 fennel bulb, thinly sliced
1 onion, finely chopped
2 garlic cloves, finely chopped
½ tsp cayenne pepper
240ml/8fl oz white wine
240ml/8fl oz clam juice
400g/14oz can chopped
   tomatoes
240ml/8fl oz water
3 strips of orange zest
1 bay leaf
½ tsp dried thyme
450g/1lb monkfish tail, dark
   membrane removed,
   flesh cut into 2.5cm/1in
   pieces
12 mussels, scrubbed and
   debearded
450g/1lb cod fillet, cut into
   2.5cm/1in pieces
450g/1lb prawns, shelled

salt and freshly ground black
   pepper to taste
2 tbsp chopped fresh parsley

METHOD
1. Heat the olive oil in a large saucepan over a medium heat. Add the leeks, fennel and onion and cook for 15 minutes, stirring occasionally, or until the vegetables are tender. Add the garlic and cayenne pepper and cook for a further 30 seconds.
2. Add the white wine and bring to boiling point. Cook for 1 minute.
3. Stir in the clam juice, tomatoes, water, orange zest, bay leaf and thyme. Press the tomatoes against the side of the pan with the back of a spoon to help break them up.
4. Bring the mixture to the boil,

then reduce the heat and simmer for 20 minutes. Discard the bay leaf.

5. Increase the heat and add the monkfish. Cover and cook for 3 minutes.

6. Stir in the mussels, cover, and cook for 1 minute.

7. Stir in the cod and prawns, cover and cook until the mussels open and the fish and prawns are cooked through. Discard any mussels that have not opened. Season to taste with salt and pepper.

8. To serve the bouillabaisse, spoon into large, shallow bowls and sprinkle the chopped parsley over each.

Bouillabaisse is traditionally served with toasted French bread and *aioli*, or garlic mayonnaise. See the recipe, right, for how to make fresh *aioli*.

AIOLI

3 garlic cloves
½ tsp salt
1 egg yolk
175ml/6fl oz olive oil

- Hold a pestle and mortar under hot running water until they feel warm to the touch, then dry with kitchen paper.
- Put the garlic and salt in the mortar and smash with the pestle until a smooth paste is formed.
- Again using the pestle, incorporate the egg yolk and continue mixing until you have a smooth paste.
- Drizzle the olive oil into the garlic paste a little at a time, stirring continuously, until you have a creamy sauce.
- Adjust the seasoning if necessary.

CHICKEN NOODLE SOUP

This soup is ideal if you are feeling a little under the weather and need a quick pick-me-up.

INGREDIENTS *Serves 6*
2 litres/3½ pints chicken stock
    (see p.12)
4 celery sticks, diced
1 onion, chopped
5 carrots, diced
4 garlic cloves, crushed
2 bay leaves
small bunch of fresh thyme
1 tbsp chopped fresh parsley
450g/1lb cooked chicken meat,
    shredded
198g/7oz can sweetcorn kernels
salt and freshly ground black
    pepper, to taste
150g/5½oz rice noodles
2 tbsp snipped chives, to garnish

METHOD
1. In a large saucepan, combine the chicken stock, celery, onion, carrots, garlic and fresh herbs. Bring to the boil, then reduce the heat and simmer for about 1 hour, covered, or until the vegetables are tender.

2. Remove the bay leaves and thyme and add the chicken and sweetcorn. Simmer for 30 minutes then season with salt and pepper to taste.

3. Bring the soup back to the boil, add the rice noodles and cook for about 15–20 minutes or as suggested on the packet.

4. Serve piping hot with a few snipped chives scattered on top.

CHICKEN, TOMATO & BEAN SOUP

If long dark evenings are getting you down, make a batch of this
soup to chase away the winter blues.

INGREDIENTS *Serves 4*

4 rashers smoked streaky
    bacon, diced
1 onion, chopped
2 garlic cloves, crushed
750ml/1¼ pints chicken stock
    (see p.12)
2 × 400g/14oz cans cannellini
    beans, drained and rinsed
115g/4oz cooked chicken breast,
    diced
400g/14oz can chopped tomatoes
120ml/4fl oz red wine
1 tbsp chopped fresh parsley
½ tsp dried basil
½ tsp dried oregano
salt and freshly ground black
    pepper, to taste
freshly grated Parmesan cheese,
    to garnish

METHOD

1. Fry the bacon in a large
saucepan over a medium heat
until it starts to release its fat –
this should take about 3–4
minutes.

2. Add the onion and garlic to
the bacon and cook for about
5 minutes or until the bacon
is crisp.

3. Add the remaining ingredients,
with the exception of the salt and
pepper and Parmesan, and bring
to the boil. Reduce the heat to
low and simmer, uncovered, for
15 minutes or until the flavours
have mingled nicely.

4. Season with salt and pepper
to taste and serve in individual
bowls with plenty of freshly
grated Parmesan sprinkled over
each one.

COCK-A-LEEKIE

As cock-a-leekie broth is thin, this soup just qualifies as 'clear'.
In Scotland it is served as a starter on Burns Night.

INGREDIENTS *Serves 6*

1 chicken, weighing 1.35kg/3lb
1 carrot, diced
1 onion, chopped
2 celery sticks, diced
1 bouquet garni
150g/6oz raw minced chicken
2 egg whites
salt and freshly ground black
    pepper, to taste
1 leek, white parts only, thinly
    sliced
15 prunes, cut into strips, to serve

METHOD

1. Roast the chicken in a
preheated oven at 200°C/400°F/
gas mark 6 for 30 minutes or until
the skin is golden brown.
2. Transfer the chicken to a large
saucepan and scatter over the
carrot, onion, celery and bouquet
garni. Pour in sufficient cold
water to cover the chicken. Bring
to the boil, then reduce the heat
and simmer for 45–50 minutes, or
until the chicken is tender.
3. Lift the chicken out of the
stock and leave to cool slightly
on a plate. Remove all the meat
from the carcass and cut into
small pieces.
4. Strain the stock through a fine
sieve, discarding the vegetables.
Put the strained stock into
a clean pan, mix in the raw
minced chicken and egg whites
and whisk the mixture quickly.
Gradually bring the stock to a
simmer. As it reaches the correct
temperature, the egg whites
and chicken will solidify on the
surface, clarifying the stock.
5. Strain the stock once more
through a fine sieve. Return to
a clean pan and bring back to
simmering point. Season to taste
with salt and black pepper.

6. Blanch the leek in boiling salted water for 2 minutes, then drain. Refresh by plunging into ice-cold water and then drain again.

7. To serve the cock-a-leekie put some shredded chicken, leek and prunes into individual serving bowls and pour the hot stock over the top.

HAGGIS

As cock-a-leekie is served before the haggis course on Burns Night, here is a recipe for haggis for those brave enough to have a go!

1 sheep's stomach
heart and lungs of 1 lamb
450g/1lb lamb trimmings
2 onions, finely chopped
225g/8oz oatmeal
1 tbsp salt

1 tsp ground black pepper
1 tsp dried coriander
1 tsp mace
1 tsp nutmeg
stock from trimmings

Clean the stomach thoroughly and soak overnight. In the morning, turn it inside out. Place the heart and lungs in a large pan of cold water with the lamb trimmings and bring to the boil. Reduce the heat and cook for 2 hours. Strain the stock through a fine sieve and set aside. Mince the heart, lungs and trimmings. Put the mince into a bowl and add the onion, oatmeal and seasoning. Mix well and add enough of the stock to moisten the mixture. Spoon into the sheep's stomach to half full and sew it up with a strong thread. Put the haggis in a pan of boiling water (just enough to cover it) and cook for 3 hours, uncovered. Serve with 'neeps and tatties'.

CLEAR TOMATO SOUP

This clear tomato soup is probably better known as consommé.
It has a delicate flavour of tomatoes and herbs.

INGREDIENTS *Serves 6*

FOR THE TOMATO SAUCE:

2 tbsp extra virgin olive oil

2 shallots, finely chopped

1 garlic clove, crushed

350g/1lb tomatoes, skinned, deseeded and chopped

10 fresh basil leaves

salt and freshly ground black pepper, to taste

FOR THE CONSOMMÉ:

1 litre/1¾ pints water

tomato sauce (see above)

250g/9oz fresh tomatoes, chopped

6 basil leaves

3 egg whites

1 tsp sugar

METHOD FOR THE SAUCE

1. Start by making the basic tomato sauce. Heat the olive oil in a small pan over a medium heat and fry the shallots gently until they are soft but not browned.

2. Add the garlic and cook for a further minute.

3. Add the tomatoes and basil and cook for 10 minutes or until the mixture has thickened. Season to taste with salt and black pepper.

METHOD FOR THE CONSOMMÉ

1. Stir the water into the tomato sauce in a large saucepan.

2. In a food processor, blend the fresh tomatoes with the basil leaves until smooth. Add the egg whites and sugar and process again until all the ingredients are mixed well.

3. Add the tomato blend from the food processor to the saucepan and bring to the boil, making sure you whisk vigorously all the time. Reduce the heat and simmer gently for 15 minutes or until you notice a crust starting to form on the surface – this is a sign that the egg whites are starting to coagulate.

4. Line a fine sieve with a piece of clean muslin that has been washed in plain water (if you use a detergent to wash muslin it can taint the delicate flavour of the consommé) and place it over a clean bowl or saucepan. Carefully lift the crust from the surface of the soup and lay it in the muslin. Gently spoon the soup over the crust and leave it to drip until there are no more juices running through. Do not be tempted to press the ingredients at this stage or your soup will be cloudy.

5. Once the soup has passed through the muslin, transfer it to a clean saucepan. Gently reheat, but do not allow it to come to the boil. Serve it warm rather than hot, as this makes the flavour more intense. Test for seasoning before serving and adjust if necessary.

VARIATION

This alternative recipe for tomato sauce takes longer to cook but has a greater depth of flavour.

1 celery stick, chopped
1 carrot, chopped
1 small onion, chopped
750g/1lb 10oz fresh tomatoes
1 tbsp chopped fresh
    parsley
1 tbsp shredded fresh basil
2 tbsp olive oil
30g/1oz unsalted butter

Put all the ingredients, with the exception of the butter, into a large saucepan and cook over a medium heat for 1 hour. Blend in a food processor until thick and chunky, then return to the saucepan. Add the butter and reduce the sauce until it has thickened slightly.

DUCK & NOODLE SOUP

Duck is the perfect meat to accompany these chunky udon noodles as it absorbs all the lovely fusion flavours.

INGREDIENTS *Serves 4*

2 duck breasts, skin on
3 tbsp fish sauce
2 tbsp soft brown sugar
1 litre/1¾ pints chicken stock
    (see p.12)
2.5cm/1in fresh root ginger, sliced
1 red chilli, deseeded and
    thinly sliced
2 spring onions, sliced on the
    diagonal (reserving some for
    garnish)
4 baby pak choi
salt and freshly ground black
    pepper, to taste
100g/3½oz udon noodles
small bunch of fresh coriander,
    roughly torn, to garnish

METHOD

1. Take the duck breasts, score the skin and marinate with 1 tbsp of fish sauce and 1 tbsp of sugar for a few hours or overnight.

2. Heat a non-stick frying pan and fry the marinated duck breasts, skin-side down. Reduce the heat to low and cook for 8 minutes to release all the fat. Turn the duck breasts over and sear for 3 minutes. Remove from the pan and set aside.

3. Heat the chicken stock in a large saucepan with the remaining fish sauce and sugar. Add the ginger, chilli, spring onions and pak choi and cook for 2 minutes. Check the flavour and add salt and pepper to taste.

4. Boil the noodles in salted water until *al dente*, then drain and divide between four large bowls. Pour the soup over the noodles, then arrange the thinly sliced duck breasts on top.

5. Sprinkle each bowl of soup with coriander and the rest of the spring onion slices.

FISH SOUP

You can use any type of fish to make this deliciously rich and pungent soup.

INGREDIENTS *Serves 4*

1 litre/1¾ pints fish stock (see p.15)

3 tbsp soy sauce

3 tbsp rice vinegar

1 tsp wasabi

1 lemongrass stalk, finely shredded

2.5cm/1in fresh root ginger, finely shredded

small handful of coriander stalks and leaves

1 red chilli, deseeded and finely sliced

450g/1lb monkfish, dark membrane removed, cut into small pieces

1 carrot, cut into matchsticks

2 spring onions, finely sliced

60g/2oz Chinese mooli radish, finely sliced

100g/3½oz cooked and peeled prawns

salt and freshly ground black pepper, to taste

METHOD

1. Put the stock, soy sauce, rice vinegar, wasabi, lemongrass, ginger, coriander and chilli into a large saucepan and bring to the boil. Reduce the heat and simmer for 10 minutes.

2. Add the monkfish, carrot, spring onions and mooli and cook for 3–4 minutes.

3. At the last minute, add the prawns and cook until they are heated through. Season the soup to taste with salt and pepper then serve immediately in individual bowls.

FRENCH ONION SOUP

The true sweet taste of the onions comes through in this classic French recipe. Eaten with French bread topped with melted Gruyère cheese, it makes a truly satisfying meal.

INGREDIENTS *Serves 4*

60g/2oz butter

1kg/2¼lb onions, finely sliced

2 garlic cloves, finely sliced

1 litre/1¾ pints vegetable stock (see p.14)

240ml/8fl oz dry red wine

1 tsp dried thyme

¼ tsp grated nutmeg

¼ tsp ground caraway seeds

1 baguette

60g/2oz Gruyère cheese

salt and freshly ground black pepper, to taste

1 tbsp chopped fresh parsley, to garnish

METHOD

1. Melt the butter in a large saucepan over medium heat, add the chopped onions and cook, stirring, until they are soft and starting to go a golden colour. Add the garlic and cook for a further minute.

2. Pour in the stock and wine and add the thyme, nutmeg and caraway. Bring the stock to boiling point, then reduce the heat and simmer gently for 30 minutes.

3. While the soup is cooking, cut the baguette into 8 slices and grill them on one side. Lay some slices of Gruyère cheese on the uncooked side and grill until the cheese has melted.

4. Season the soup with salt and pepper to taste, then spoon into individual bowls. Float 2 pieces of bread on the surface of each bowl of soup and finish with a liberal sprinkling of chopped parsley.

HOT & SOUR SCALLOP SOUP

With their tender, sweet flesh, scallops perfectly complement
the hot and sour broth in this soup.

INGREDIENTS *Serves 4*

600ml/1 pint fish stock (see p.15)

125g/4½oz chestnut mushrooms,
  sliced

1 lemon grass stalk, cut into
  2.5cm/1in strips

3 hot green chillies, deseeded
  and thinly sliced

2 garlic cloves, finely sliced

3 kaffir lime leaves

1 tsp ground galangal or ginger

2 tbsp fish sauce

20 fresh scallops

lime juice, to taste

fresh coriander leaves, to garnish

METHOD

1. Pour the fish stock into a
large saucepan and bring to
the boil. Reduce the heat so
that it is simmering and add
the mushrooms, lemon grass,
chillies, garlic, lime leaves,
galangal and about 1 tablespoon
of the fish sauce. Cook gently for
about 4 minutes.

2. Add the scallops and cook for
a further 3–4 minutes or until they
are cooked through.

3. Remove the lemon grass,
season to taste with extra fish
sauce and lime juice and serve
immediately in individual bowls.

PREPARING SCALLOPS

If you are using scallops
that are still in the shell, run
a flexible knife over the flat
side of the shell to open it.
Remove the scallop with a
spoon, pull off the frill and
black stomach sac and
discard. Rinse thoroughly
under cold water.

LAMB & CABBAGE SOUP

Although this soup is clear, it is full of chunky vegetables and meat which make it a filling supper dish.

INGREDIENTS *Serves 4*

2 tbsp olive oil

400g/14oz lean leg of lamb, cut
    into 2.5cm/1in cubes

1 onion, chopped

2 garlic cloves, finely chopped

1 litre/1¾ pints chicken stock
    (see p.12)

2 large potatoes, peeled
    and diced

½ small white cabbage,
    shredded

1 carrot, diced

200g/7oz pumpkin or butternut
    squash flesh, diced

200g/7oz cauliflower, broken into
    small florets

2.5cm/1in fresh root ginger,
    peeled and grated

1 tsp chilli powder

salt and freshly ground black
    pepper, to taste

2 tbsp chopped fresh dill,
    to garnish

METHOD

1. Heat the oil in a large
saucepan over a medium heat.
Add the meat and brown on all
sides. Add the onion and garlic
and fry for 2 minutes.

2. Stir in the stock, then add
the potatoes, cabbage, carrot,
pumpkin, cauliflower and ginger
and bring to the boil. Reduce
the heat, cover, and simmer
for 45–60 minutes, or until the
vegetables are tender and the
lamb is cooked.

3. Add the chilli powder and
season to taste with salt and
pepper before serving. Spoon
into individual bowls and
sprinkle with fresh dill.

OXTAIL SOUP

Oxtail soup has a wonderfully rich and indulgent flavour which leaves a warm, peppery feeling on the tongue.

INGREDIENTS *Serves 4*

60g/2oz butter

1 tbsp olive oil

1 large oxtail, trimmed of fat and cut into pieces

1 onion, with skin, halved

4 celery sticks, chopped

2 carrots, chopped

5 garlic cloves, roughly chopped

8 black peppercorns

1 bouquet garni

2 litres/3½ pints water

4 tbsp dry sherry

salt and freshly ground black pepper, to taste

METHOD

1. Melt the butter and oil in a large saucepan and add the oxtail pieces. Cook over a medium heat until the oxtail is browned on all sides.

2. Add the vegetables and cook for 2–3 minutes, turning them in the cooking juices.

3. Add the peppercorns, bouquet garni and water and bring to the boil. Turn the heat right down, cover the pan and simmer gently for about 3 hours or until the meat is falling off the bone.

4. Strain the cooking liquid through a fine sieve, reserving the meat and discarding the vegetables. Put the stock in the refrigerator, covered, and leave it overnight to chill.

5. When cool enough to handle, take all the meat from the bone, season with salt and pepper and store overnight in the refrigerator.

6. The following morning, remove the jellied fat from the top of the stock and discard it. Put the stock into a saucepan, add the meat and the sherry and reheat until piping hot. Check the seasoning and serve.

MIXED BEAN SOUP

This soup is economical and delicious; the combination of different beans gives it a unique flavour.

INGREDIENTS *Serves 4*

400g/14oz dried bean mix
   (cannellini, kidney and butter
   beans, brown, green and red
   lentils, and split peas)
1 tbsp olive oil
1 onion, chopped
2 celery sticks, chopped
2 garlic cloves, finely chopped
1 tsp ground cumin
1 tsp hot chilli powder
1 bouquet garni
2 tomatoes, skinned, seeded and
   chopped
600ml/1 pint chicken stock
   (see p.12)
1 ham hock
1 tbsp red wine vinegar
1 tbsp chopped fresh parsley
salt and freshly ground black
   pepper, to taste

METHOD

1. Put all the beans in a large bowl, cover with water and soak overnight.

2. Heat the olive oil in a large saucepan over a medium heat before adding the onion, celery and garlic. Sauté until the onion is soft but not browned. Add the cumin and chilli powder and cook for a further minute.

3. Add the bouquet garni, tomatoes and chicken stock. Drain the beans and add to the soup, together with the ham hock and vinegar. Bring the soup to a boil, then reduce the heat to a gentle simmer. Cook for 1½–2 hours to give sufficient time for all the flavours to infuse. Remove any scum with a slotted spoon.

4. Just before serving, remove the bouquet garni and ham hock, stir in the chopped parsley and season to taste with salt and black pepper.

MIXED VEGETABLE & CHICKEN SOUP

A very simple but delicious soup, packed full of flavour from all the different vegetables in a light stock.

INGREDIENTS *Serves 4*

30g/2oz butter

1 onion, chopped

2 leeks, white parts only, cut into
1cm/½in slices

1 carrot, sliced

400g/14oz potato, peeled
and diced

400g/14oz celeriac, peeled
and diced

1 fennel bulb, sliced

1 small parsnip, sliced

750ml/1¼ pints chicken or
vegetable stock (see pp.12
and 14)

1 sprig of fresh rosemary

225g/8oz cooked chicken, cut into
small pieces

salt and freshly ground black
pepper, to taste

finely chopped parsley and
crunchy bacon bits, to garnish

METHOD

1. Melt the butter in a large saucepan over a medium heat and add the onion. Sauté until the onion is soft but not browned. Add the remaining vegetables and cook for a further 3–4 minutes, or until the vegetables have started to soften.

2. Add the chicken or vegetable stock and sprig of fresh rosemary and bring to the boil. Reduce the heat, cover, and simmer for 20–30 minutes or until the vegetables are tender.

3. Add the chicken pieces and cook for a further 4–5 minutes or until the chicken is warmed through.

4. Remove the sprig of rosemary and season to taste with salt and pepper. Serve in individual bowls with chopped parsley and crunchy bacon bits.

MUSHROOM SOUP WITH RAVIOLI

The beauty of this soup is that you can fill your homemade ravioli with any ingredients you like. You will find that children love it.

INGREDIENTS *Serves 4*
1 litre/1¾ pints chicken stock
(see p.12)
120ml/4fl oz dry white wine
2 shallots, finely chopped
30g/1oz dried porcini mushrooms
60g/2oz unsalted butter
350g/12oz assorted mushrooms
(such as ceps, crimini, shiitake,
oyster), finely sliced
salt and freshly ground black
pepper, to taste
chopped fresh chervil or parsley,
to garnish

FOR THE RAVIOLI:
400g/14oz plain flour
4 eggs
1 tsp olive oil
1 tsp salt

FOR THE FILLING:
1 tbsp olive oil
1 onion, finely chopped

200g/7oz chestnut mushrooms
250g/9oz ricotta cheese
60g/2oz pecorino cheese, grated
½ tsp grated nutmeg
115g/4oz baby spinach leaves,
wilted
salt and freshly ground black
pepper, to taste

METHOD FOR THE SOUP
1. Pour the chicken stock
and white wine into a large
saucepan, add the shallots and
dried porcini mushrooms and
bring to the boil. Remove from
the heat, cover, and leave to
stand for 30 minutes.
2. Drain the stock through
some clean muslin, reserving
the porcini mushrooms but
discarding the shallots.
3. Pour the stock into a clean
saucepan and chop the porcini
mushrooms.

4. Heat the butter in a frying pan and fry the assorted mushrooms on both sides until they are soft and golden brown. Season with salt and black pepper. Add the mushrooms, including the porcini, to the stock in the saucepan.

METHOD FOR THE RAVIOLI

1. Combine the flour, eggs, oil and salt in a bowl and knead with your hands until you have a smooth dough. Roll it into a ball, cover with cling film and leave to rest for 30 minutes.

2. While the dough is resting, prepare the filling for the ravioli. Heat the oil in a frying pan, add the chopped onion and sauté until soft. Add the mushrooms and cook over a medium heat until all the liquid from the mushrooms has evaporated. Set aside to cool.

3. Mix together the ricotta and pecorino cheeses, nutmeg and wilted spinach leaves and season with salt and pepper to taste.

4. Remove the cling film from the dough and knead the dough for a few minutes. Roll it out very thinly on a lightly floured surface. Cut it in two and, on one half, place heaped teaspoons of filling with 4cm/1½in spaces between them. Dampen the edges, then cover with the other ravioli sheet, pressing down firmly around each mound of filling. Use a pastry cutter to cut out the individual ravioli.

To finish the soup, bring the mushroom stock back to the boil and add the ravioli. Cover and cook for 3–4 minutes. Ladle the soup into individual bowls and garnish with either chopped chervil or parsley.

MUSSEL SOUP

This has all the freshness of the sea, with a lovely spicy broth to give a touch of the Mediterranean.

INGREDIENTS *Serves 4*

3 tbsp olive oil

3 red chillies, finely sliced

1 onion, finely chopped

6 garlic cloves, finely chopped

2 large tomatoes, skinned
    and chopped

2.5cm/1in fresh root ginger,
    peeled and grated

2 tbsp fish sauce

120ml/4fl oz white wine

500ml/16fl oz water

1.35kg/3lb mussels, scrubbed,
    rinsed and beards removed

salt and freshly ground black
    pepper, to taste

small bunch of fresh coriander
    leaves, to garnish

METHOD

1. Heat the olive oil in a large saucepan over a medium heat, add the chopped chillies, onion and garlic and sauté until they are soft but not browned.

2. Add the tomatoes, ginger and fish sauce and sauté for 2 minutes or until the tomatoes start to soften.

3. Add the wine and water and bring to the boil. Add the mussels, reduce the heat, cover and simmer for about 10 minutes or until the mussels open. Discard any shells that haven't opened and season to taste with salt and pepper. Garnish with coriander and serve piping hot, with some slices of bruschetta to dip into the mussel broth.

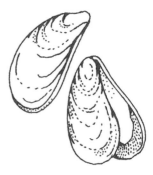

PRAWN & VERMICELLI SOUP

This soup is spiced up with the addition of chilli oil just before serving. You can adjust the amount of heat by using more or less seasoning.

INGREDIENTS *Serves 4*

20 large prawns, shelled and
    deveined
1 tsp salt
1 tsp freshly ground black pepper
1 tsp cornflour
2 tbsp olive oil
1 onion, finely chopped
3 garlic cloves, crushed
1 sweet red pepper, deseeded
    and cut into thin strips
250ml/8fl oz chicken stock
    (see p.12)
85g/3oz vermicelli, soaked
1 tbsp finely chopped fresh
    coriander
chilli oil, to taste
salt and freshly ground black
    pepper, to taste

METHOD

1. Season the prawns with salt and pepper and toss in the cornflour. Leave for 10 minutes.

2. Heat 1 tablespoon of oil in a large frying pan or wok over a high heat and stir fry the prawns for about 3–4 minutes or until cooked. Remove with a slotted spoon and set aside.

3. Heat the remaining oil in the same pan and sauté the onion, garlic and red pepper until the onion is translucent. Stir in the prawns and mix well.

4. Pour the chicken stock into a large saucepan, add the vermicelli and bring to the boil. Cook for 2–3 minutes, then add the reserved prawns and vegetables. Heat through for a further minute.

5. Add the chopped coriander, stir in some chilli oil and season to taste with salt and pepper before serving.

TURKEY, SPINACH & SPAGHETTI SOUP

This is a good recipe for using up any leftover turkey after the indulgences of Christmas day.

INGREDIENTS *Serves 4–6*

1 tbsp olive oil
1 onion, chopped
2.5cm/1in fresh root ginger,
   peeled and grated
1 garlic clove, crushed
1 tsp finely chopped fresh sage
1 litre/1¾ pints chicken stock
   (see p.12)
450g/1lb boneless turkey, skinned
   and cut into chunks
400g/14oz spaghetti, uncooked
30g/1 oz butter
350g/12oz baby spinach leaves
lemon juice, to taste
salt and freshly ground black
   pepper, to taste

METHOD

1. Heat the oil in a large saucepan over a medium heat and fry the onion and ginger for 3–4 minutes or until the onion is translucent. Add the garlic and sage and

cook for a further minute.

2. Pour the stock into the pan and add the turkey and spaghetti. Bring to the boil, cover, and reduce the heat to simmering point. Cook for about 15 minutes or until the spaghetti is *al dente*.

3. In a separate pan, melt the butter and briefly wilt the spinach. Add the spinach to the soup and season to taste with lemon juice and salt and pepper. Serve immediately with chunks of fresh bread.

PART 5

CHILLED SOUPS

There is a host of delicious soups that can be served chilled straight from the fridge. They make a refreshing change from salads as a light meal in summer.

MAKING CHILLED SOUPS

A chilled soup makes a light and delicious summer lunch. Just as
hot soups warm you up during the cold winter months,
a refreshing chilled soup will cool you down
during the warm days of summer.

Chilled soups can be served
as a starter, a main course or a
side dish to accompany maybe
a salad or a cheese platter with
bread. Probably the best-known
of all chilled soups is the Spanish
gazpacho, a tomato-based
creation with a long list
of ingredients to add texture
and flavour.

Many of the vegetables, herbs
and spices used in hot soups can
be adapted to make a delicious
cold soup. However, you need
to remember that a cold soup
will lose a little of its spiciness
through the chilling process, so
if you are adapting a recipe for
hot soup you should compensate
by adding extra flavour. As
before, always use the freshest

possible ingredients and explore
new combinations of flavours by
adding spices or herbs.

Chilled soups can be topped
with many different titbits, for
example, fresh herbs, soured
cream, croutons, yogurt, or even
whipped cream. Leave the
seasoning to the end so that you
can adjust it to your taste.

If a recipe requires blending
to a smooth consistency, as many
chilled soups do, you can use
either a traditional blender or
a hand (immersion) blender –
both work equally well. With a
traditional blender, you may find
you have to process the soup in
batches, whereas a hand blender
can be used in the saucepan and
the blending done in one go.

ASPARAGUS SOUP

In this chilled soup, even the woody ends of the asparagus spears do not go to waste – they are used to flavour the stock.

INGREDIENTS *Serves 4*

450g/1lb fresh asparagus spears
1 litre/1¾ pints chicken stock
 (see p.14)
30g/1oz butter
1 large onion, chopped
1 leek, white parts only, finely
 sliced
1 tsp finely chopped fresh savory
 (or ½ tsp dried)
salt and freshly ground black
 pepper, to taste
150ml/5fl oz single cream
grated lemon zest, to garnish

METHOD

1. Break the woody ends from the asparagus spears, place them in a large saucepan with the chicken stock and bring to a vigorous simmer. Cook for 1 hour, then drain through a fine sieve and discard the solids.

2. Melt the butter in a large frying pan, add the onion and leek and sauté until the onion is translucent but not browned.

3. Add the onion and leek to the drained stock in a clean saucepan and bring to a boil. Reduce the heat then add the asparagus tips and cook for about 5 minutes or until the asparagus is just tender.

4. Pour the soup into a blender and process until you have a smooth purée. Transfer the soup to a large bowl and season with the savory and salt and black pepper to taste.

5. Add the cream and stir well. Refrigerate for about 4 hours before serving, garnished with the grated lemon zest.

If you want a slightly tangier flavour, replace the cream with buttermilk.

AVOCADO SOUP

This must be the perfect chilled soup for summer, as it requires no cooking whatsoever.

INGREDIENTS *Serves 4*

4 ripe avocados, stoned, peeled and chopped

1 cucumber, peeled, deseeded and chopped

2 spring onions, finely chopped

250ml/8fl oz chilled vegetable stock (see p.14)

120ml/4fl oz soured cream

2 tbsp chopped fresh coriander leaves

½ tsp cayenne pepper

salt and freshly ground black pepper, to taste

METHOD

1. Put the avocado flesh, cucumber and spring onions into a blender with the vegetable stock and process until it is smooth.

2. Stir in the soured cream, fresh coriander and cayenne pepper and season to taste with salt and pepper. Chill in the refrigerator for 2 hours before serving in individual bowls.

CHEF'S TIP

The easiest way to remove the flesh from an avocado is to cut lengthways through the skin and flesh to the depth of the stone with a sharp knife. Grip both sides of the avocado firmly and twist apart. Remove the stone with a spoon and score the flesh in several places. Scoop out the flesh with a spoon or, if you want slices, cut several times lengthways with a sharp knife and carefully separate the wedges from the skin.

BORSCHT

Borscht is a Ukrainian national soup and gets its name from the old Slavic word *br'sch*, meaning 'beet'. There are many variations on this recipe; this one uses soured cream.

INGREDIENTS *Serves 4*

60g/2oz butter
1 onion, chopped
1 garlic clove, finely chopped
100g/3½oz white cabbage, shredded
1 carrot, grated
100g/3½oz leek, thinly sliced
750g/1lb 10oz fresh beetroot, peeled and grated
6 black peppercorns
2 bay leaves
750ml/1¼ pints vegetable stock (see p.14)
200g/7oz soured cream
1 tbsp white wine vinegar
salt and freshly ground black pepper, to taste

METHOD

1. Heat the butter in a large saucepan over a medium heat. Add the onion and garlic and sauté for about 5 minutes or until the onion is translucent but not browned. Add the cabbage, carrot, leek, beetroot, peppercorns and bay leaves and cook for a further 2 minutes.

2. Add the vegetable stock and bring to a boil. Reduce the heat, cover the pan, and simmer for 20 minutes.

3. Remove the bay leaves, pour the soup into a blender and process until you have a purée.

4. Pour the soup into a large bowl and stir in the soured cream. Season with white wine vinegar and salt and pepper to taste.

As a variation on the above, try using raspberry vinegar instead of white wine vinegar and add 1 tbsp grated horseradish.

CARROT & GINGER SOUP

This soup is lovely served chilled with some bread sticks and a glass of cold white wine.

INGREDIENTS *Serves 4*

2 tbsp olive oil

2 onions, chopped

1 leek, white parts only, finely sliced

3 garlic cloves, finely chopped

5 carrots, sliced

1 sweet potato, peeled and diced

4cm/1½in fresh root ginger, grated

900ml/1½ pints vegetable stock (see p.14)

400ml/14fl oz can coconut milk

1 tsp sweet paprika

1 tsp turmeric

salt and freshly ground black pepper, to taste

roasted sunflower seeds or pine nuts, to garnish

METHOD

1. Heat the olive oil in a large saucepan over a medium heat. Add the onions and sauté for about 4 minutes. Add the leek and garlic and sauté for a further 5 minutes or until softened, but not browned.

2. Add the carrots and cook for about 6 minutes, stirring occasionally, or until the carrots start to caramelize slightly.

3. Add the sweet potato, ginger, stock and coconut milk and bring to a gentle boil. Reduce the heat, add the paprika and turmeric and then simmer, covered, for about 30–35 minutes or until the vegetables are soft.

4. Pour the soup into a blender and process until smooth and velvety in texture. Transfer to a large bowl. Taste for seasoning and place in the refrigerator for at least 4 hours before serving.

5. To serve, pour into 4 bowls and garnish with a few roasted sunflower seeds or pine nuts.

CARROT, CUMIN & LIME SOUP

Carrot adds a delightfully sweet flavour to chilled soups and can be combined with many different ingredients.

INGREDIENTS *Serves 4*

2 tbsp olive oil

900g/2lb carrots, chopped

2 leeks, white parts only, sliced

2 garlic cloves, finely chopped

3 tsp ground cumin

½ tsp dried chilli flakes

1.2 litres/2 pints chicken or vegetable stock (see pp.12 and 14)

120ml/4fl oz soured cream

2 tbsp fresh lime juice

salt and freshly ground black pepper, to taste

2 tbsp chopped fresh coriander

2 tsp grated lime zest

METHOD

1. Heat the olive oil in a large saucepan over a medium heat. Add the carrots and leeks and sauté for about 5 minutes or until they are softened but not browned.

2. Add the garlic and sauté for a further minute.

3. Add the cumin and chilli flakes and cook for another 30 seconds.

4. Add the stock and bring to the boil. Reduce the heat and cook, uncovered, for about 30–35 minutes or until the vegetables are soft.

5. Pour the soup into a blender and process until you have a purée. Transfer to a clean bowl. Allow the soup to cool and then whisk in the soured cream.

6. Place the soup in the refrigerator and chill for at least 4 hours. Just before serving, stir in the lime juice and season to taste with salt and pepper.

7. Serve chilled in individual bowls with chopped coriander and grated lime zest as a garnish. Add more chilli flakes for those who like it spicy.

CREAMY BROCCOLI SOUP

This rich, creamy soup tastes really good when chilled;
as broccoli is rich in nutrients, it's good for you, too.

INGREDIENTS *Serves 4*

1 litre/1¾ pints chicken stock
(see p.12)
1 large onion, finely chopped
1 garlic clove, finely chopped
450g/1lb broccoli heads, broken
into small florets
2 tsp dried thyme
2 bay leaves
60g/2oz butter
1 tbsp plain flour
400ml/14fl oz whole milk
salt and freshly ground black
pepper, to taste
soured cream and bacon bits, to
garnish

METHOD

1. Put the stock, onion, garlic,
broccoli, thyme and bay leaves
in a large saucepan and bring to
the boil.
2. Reduce the heat, cover the
pan, and simmer for 10–15
minutes or until the broccoli
is tender.
3. Remove the bay leaves and
pour the soup into a blender.
Cover and process for about
1 minute or until completely
smooth. Pour into a large bowl.
4. Melt the butter in a small
saucepan and stir in the flour,
cooking until the mixture starts to
come away from the sides of the
pan. Gradually incorporate the
milk, stirring constantly, until the
mixture thickens.
5. Pour the white sauce into the
broccoli mixture in the bowl
and stir thoroughly to combine.
Check the flavour and add salt
and pepper to taste. Place in the
refrigerator and leave to chill for
at least 3–4 hours.
6. Serve in individual bowls with
a swirl of soured cream and
some crispy fried bacon bits.

COURGETTE SOUP

This fresh-tasting soup combines courgette, tomato, mint and basil with a hint of lemon.

INGREDIENTS *Serves 4*

3 tbsp olive oil

1 onion, finely chopped

4 tomatoes, skinned, deseeded
and chopped

1 litre/1¾ pints water

8 sprigs of fresh mint

3 courgettes, sliced

1 tbsp cornflour

salt and freshly ground black
pepper, to taste

2 tsp lemon juice

2 sprigs of fresh basil

METHOD

1. Heat 2 tablespoons of the olive oil in a large saucepan over a medium heat and sauté the onion until it is translucent but not browned.

2. Add the chopped tomatoes and cook for a further 2 minutes, stirring continuously.

3. Add the water to the pan and bring to the boil. Add 4 sprigs of fresh mint and the courgettes, reduce the heat and allow the soup to simmer for 15 minutes, covered.

4. Discard the mint sprigs and dissolve the cornflour in a little cold water. Add this paste to the soup and stir constantly over a high heat until the soup has thickened. Season to taste with salt and pepper and leave to cool.

5. Chill in the refrigerator for at least 3–4 hours. Just before serving, season with the lemon juice and garnish each bowl with some fresh basil leaves and the remaining mint.

CUCUMBER & AVOCADO SOUP

It's cool, it's creamy and it has a hit of chilli – the perfect soup when you don't fancy anything hot to eat.

INGREDIENTS *Serves 4*

2 large cucumbers, peeled, deseeded and chopped

1 avocado, peeled, stoned and chopped

3 spring onions, chopped

1 serrano chilli, deseeded and finely chopped

250ml/8fl oz Greek yogurt

120ml/4fl oz soured cream

juice of 1 lime

2 tbsp finely chopped fresh coriander

½ tsp ground cumin

½ tsp dried oregano

1 tsp agave nectar or runny honey

salt and freshly ground black pepper, to taste

TO GARNISH:

1 tomato, skinned, deseeded and finely chopped

1 spring onion, finely chopped

1 tbsp freshly grated Parmesan cheese

METHOD

1. Place all the ingredients except the salt and pepper in a blender. Process for about 1 minute or until the mixture is thick, smooth and creamy in texture.

2. Pour the soup into a large bowl, add salt and pepper to taste and refrigerate for 3–4 hours before serving.

3. Serve in individual bowls garnished with the chopped tomato and spring onion and a generous sprinkling of Parmesan cheese.

The flavour of this soup improves with keeping. It is well worth making the soup the day before you intend to serve it.

CUCUMBER, YOGURT & MINT SOUP

If you grow your own cucumbers you will probably have
a glut in summer. This refreshing soup can
help to use them up.

INGREDIENTS *Serves 6*

900g/2lb cucumbers, peeled,
   deseeded and cut into
   5cm/2in pieces
1 small onion, chopped
1 garlic clove, finely sliced
1 jalapeño chilli, deseeded
   and chopped
8 mint leaves
2 tbsp olive oil
2 tbsp lemon juice
1 tsp sugar
1 tsp sea salt
freshly ground black pepper,
   to taste
175g/6oz plain yogurt
120ml/4fl oz water
mint leaves, to garnish

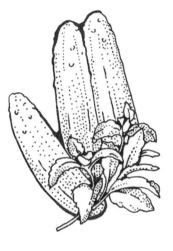

METHOD

1. Place all the ingredients
except the garnish into a blender
and pulse a few times until
everything is roughly chopped.
Turn the blender to full speed
and process until you have a
smooth, silky consistency.

2. Transfer the soup to a bowl,
check the seasoning and
refrigerate for at least 4 hours so
that it is thoroughly chilled.

3. Serve in individual bowls or
glasses and garnish with a few
small mint leaves.

GARLIC & ALMOND SOUP

This cold, creamy summer soup from Spain has a distinctive flavour of sweet garlic and almonds. It is believed to originate from the time when the Moors introduced almonds to Andalusia.

INGREDIENTS *Serves 6*

2 slices of day-old white bread (about 100g/3½oz), cut into 2.5cm/1in pieces
1.5 litres/2½ pints water
10 garlic cloves, coarsely chopped
300g/10oz almonds, blanched
2 tsp salt
120ml/4fl oz malt vinegar
120ml/4fl oz extra virgin olive oil
freshly ground black pepper, to taste
1 eating apple, peeled and thinly sliced, and toasted flaked almonds to garnish

METHOD

1. Soak the bread in 200ml/ 7fl oz of the water in a bowl for 10 minutes.
2. Put the garlic and almonds into a blender and process for about 1 minute or until the contents are finely ground. Add the soaked bread and its water, salt, vinegar and oil and blend for 2 minutes or until you have a smooth paste.
3. Transfer the paste to a glass bowl and stir in the remaining water. Cover with cling film and refrigerate for at least 4 hours.
4. Stir the soup thoroughly just before serving and add salt and pepper if necessary.
5. Ladle into individual bowls and garnish each one with slivers of apple and toasted flaked almonds.

GAZPACHO

This is probably the best-known chilled soup of all, with its fresh tomato base complemented by flavours of the Mediterranean. Give your guests a choice of toppings to go with it.

INGREDIENTS *Serves 4*

60g/2oz day-old bread

200ml/7fl oz water

4 large ripe tomatoes, skinned, deseeded and chopped

1 onion, chopped

½ sweet red pepper, deseeded and chopped

½ green pepper, deseeded and chopped

½ cucumber, peeled and chopped

3 garlic cloves, crushed

2 tbsp red wine vinegar

4 tbsp extra virgin olive oil

½ red chilli, deseeded and chopped

salt and freshly ground black pepper, to taste

FOR THE TOPPINGS:

chopped hard-boiled eggs

finely chopped onion

finely chopped red pepper

finely chopped cucumber

finely snipped chives

METHOD

1. Tear the bread into small pieces and soak it in the water for 30 minutes.

2. Squeeze the bread to remove most of the water and place it in a blender with the tomatoes, onion, red and green pepper, cucumber, garlic, vinegar, olive oil and chilli. Blend until you have a smooth consistency. If you feel the soup is too thick, add a little more water. Season to taste.

3. Pour the soup into a large glass bowl and leave in the refrigerator for several hours. Serve with bowls of toppings.

PEA & MINT SOUP

If you fancy something a little different for lunch, try this very simple recipe for fresh pea soup enhanced with the flavour of mint.

INGREDIENTS Serves 6

1 tbsp olive oil

1 large leek, finely sliced

2 garlic cloves, finely chopped

1 rasher smoked streaky bacon, chopped

500ml/16fl oz vegetable stock (see p.14)

675g/1½lb shelled fresh peas (or frozen)

1 Little Gem lettuce, washed and shredded

1 tbsp finely chopped fresh mint

½ tsp sugar

salt and freshly ground black pepper, to taste

TO GARNISH:

90ml/3fl oz double cream

a small handful of mint leaves

METHOD

1. Heat the oil in a large saucepan over a medium heat, add the leek, garlic and bacon and sauté for 5–6 minutes or until the leek is softened but not browned.

2. Pour in the stock and bring to the boil. Add the peas, bring back to the boil, then reduce the heat until the liquid is just simmering. Stir in the lettuce, mint and sugar and cook for 5 minutes or until the peas are tender.

3. Pour the soup into a food processor and blend until it is smooth. Taste and add seasoning as necessary.

4. Pour the soup into a large bowl and leave to cool. Cover and chill for 4 hours or overnight before serving.

5. Serve in cold bowls with a dollop of double cream and a few mint leaves to garnish.

PEA & SQUASH SOUP

Bright yellow summer squash is the main ingredient in this soup,
with peas adding a little extra depth of flavour.

INGREDIENTS *Serves 6*

1 litre/1¾ pints vegetable stock
(see p.14)
450g/1lb summer squash, peeled,
deseeded and chopped
1 small onion, finely chopped
225g/8oz shelled fresh peas (or
frozen)
2 garlic cloves, finely chopped
salt and freshly ground black
pepper, to taste
240ml/8fl oz natural yogurt

METHOD

1. Pour the vegetable stock into
a large saucepan and add the
summer squash, onion, peas and
garlic. Bring the mixture to a boil
then reduce the heat, cover the
pan and simmer gently for
15–20 minutes.
2. Pour the soup into a food
processor and blend until
smooth.
3. Transfer to a large bowl and
taste, adding salt and pepper
as necessary. Chill in the
refrigerator for at least 4 hours
or overnight. Serve in individual
bowls with a large spoonful of
yogurt on top of each.

Butternut squash may be
substituted for summer squash.

PUMPKIN SOUP

If you love coconut, then you will enjoy this wonderful combination of pumpkin, spices and fresh coconut.

INGREDIENTS *Serves 4*
350g/12oz pumpkin flesh
2 tbsp olive oil
salt and freshly ground black
  pepper, to taste
100g/3½oz fresh coconut flesh
  (reserve the liquid from the
  coconut, too)
1½ tsp ground cumin
1½ tsp ground coriander
3 black peppercorns
1 garlic clove, finely chopped
1 tsp red curry paste
1 tbsp ground almonds

TO GARNISH:
1 tbsp toasted pumpkin seeds
75ml/2½fl oz coconut cream
1 tbsp finely chopped fresh
  coriander

METHOD
1. Preheat the oven to 200°C/
400°F/gas mark 6.

2. Cut the pumpkin flesh into 2.5cm/1in cubes. Arrange them in a single layer on a baking tray and drizzle with the olive oil and a little salt and black pepper. Roast in the oven for 15–20 minutes or until the pumpkin is soft and just starting to brown.

3. When the pumpkin has cooled down a little, put it in a blender with the remaining ingredients. Process until the soup has a smooth, silky texture. Taste to see if you need to adjust the seasoning, adding more salt and pepper if needed.

4. Pour the soup into a large bowl and chill in the refrigerator for 2–3 hours.

5. Serve in individual bowls with a handful of toasted pumpkin seeds, a spoonful of coconut cream and a sprinkling of chopped coriander to garnish.

ROASTED AUBERGINE SOUP

Garlic and aubergine are combined in this chilled soup. The addition of cayenne pepper and lemon juice helps to add flavour.

INGREDIENTS *Serves 4–6*
450g/1lb aubergine
4 garlic cloves, cut in half
2 tbsp olive oil
salt and freshly ground black
  pepper, to taste
1 tsp cayenne pepper
1 litre/1¾ pints vegetable stock
  (see p.14)
zest of ½ lemon
juice of 1 lemon
2 tsp ground cumin

METHOD
1. Preheat the oven to 200°C/ 400°F/gas mark 6.
2. Wash the aubergines and make slits in several places with a sharp knife. Place half a garlic clove in each slit, then drizzle the aubergines with olive oil and season with salt and pepper and cayenne pepper. Put in a roasting pan and place in the oven for 40 minutes, or until the aubergines are soft and cooked through.
3. When the aubergine are cool enough to handle, cut in half and remove the seeds and garlic cloves. Scrape out the flesh from the skin with a spoon and place it in a large saucepan.
4. Add the stock, lemon zest and lemon juice and bring the mixture to a boil. Turn down the heat and simmer gently for 15 minutes.
5. Pour the soup into a blender and whizz to a purée. Pour into a bowl and taste for seasoning – if you want it spicier, add a little more cayenne pepper.
6. Dry fry the cumin in a small pan for about 1 minute or until it is fragrant. Stir the cumin into the soup, then cover the bowl and chill for 2–3 hours before serving.

CRAB AND ROASTED PEPPER SOUP

This is one of the finest chilled soups and is a great dish for a summer barbecue.

INGREDIENTS *Serves 2*

3 sweet yellow peppers, deseeded and halved
1 tbsp olive oil
400ml/14fl oz chicken stock (see p.12)
the juice of 1 orange
75ml/2½fl oz dry white wine
1 garlic clove, finely chopped
2 tsp balsamic vinegar
salt and freshly ground black pepper, to taste
115g/4oz fresh crab meat
1 tbsp finely chopped fresh parsley, to garnish

METHOD

1. Brush the skins of the peppers with olive oil and place them skin-side down on the barbecue grill (or skin-side up under the oven grill). Cook until the skin blackens and starts to blister.
2. Place the peppers in a bowl, cover with cling film and allow them to steam. When cool, peel off the skins and cut the flesh into pieces.
3. Combine the remaining ingredients, with the exception of the salt and pepper and crab meat, in a blender and process until smooth in texture.
4. Transfer the soup to a saucepan and bring to a gentle simmer, stirring occasionally. Leave it to cool to room temperature then pour into a bowl and chill in the refrigerator for 3–4 hours.
5. Add salt and pepper to taste, then serve in individual bowls with a good helping of crab meat in the centre, sprinkled with some fresh parsley.

For a truly luxurious dish to serve at dinner parties, substitute some fresh lobster for the crab meat.

ROASTED TOMATO SOUP

Roasting the tomatoes before adding them to the soup makes the flavour really rich. Served with fresh, crusty bread, this is a lovely light lunch dish or starter.

INGREDIENTS *Serves 4*

800g/1¾lb plum tomatoes, roughly chopped

1 sweet red pepper, deseeded and roughly chopped

4 garlic cloves, left whole in their skins

2 tbsp olive oil

1 litre/1¾ pints vegetable stock (see p.14)

small bunch of fresh basil leaves

salt and freshly ground black pepper, to taste

METHOD

1. Preheat the oven to 220°C/425°F/gas mark 7.

2. Arrange the chopped tomatoes, pepper and garlic in a single layer on a baking tray and drizzle with a little olive oil. Roast in the oven for 45 minutes or until the tomatoes are soft and their skins have started to blacken slightly. Once cool enough to handle, squeeze the garlic out of its papery skin.

3. Put the tomatoes, pepper and garlic flesh into a large saucepan and pour the stock over them. Add the basil leaves and bring the mixture to a boil. Reduce the heat and simmer for 3–4 minutes.

4. Allow the soup to cool, then pour it into a blender, first reserving about one-quarter of the vegetables. Blend the soup until smooth and silky in texture.

5. Pour into a bowl, season to taste with salt and pepper, cover, and chill for 2–3 hours.

6. Serve with the reserved vegetables piled in the middle of each bowl. Drizzle olive oil over some fresh bread and serve on the side.

SPICY BLACK-EYED BEAN & SWEET POTATO SOUP

There are a lot of flavours to tease the tastebuds in this spicy soup, which is delicious served hot or cold.

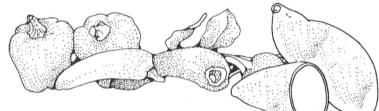

INGREDIENTS *Serves 4*

1 sweet red pepper, deseeded
   and halved
1 tbsp olive oil
1 small onion, finely chopped
2 celery sticks, thinly sliced
1 garlic clove, crushed
120ml/4fl oz water
120ml/4fl oz vegetable stock
   (see p.14)
2 plum tomatoes, skinned and
   roughly chopped
200g/7oz can black-eyed beans,
   drained and rinsed
1 large sweet potato, peeled and
   cut into chunks
1 tsp light brown sugar

1 tsp cinnamon
½ tsp cayenne pepper
1 tsp crushed red pepper flakes
1 bay leaf
¼ tsp dried thyme
¼ tsp dried basil
¼ tsp dried oregano
¼ tsp dried coriander
¼ tsp dried rosemary
¼ tsp mustard powder
¼ tsp ground cumin
salt and freshly ground black
   pepper, to taste
1 tbsp finely chopped fresh
   parsley, to garnish

METHOD

1. Brush the skin of the pepper halves with olive oil and place them skin-side up on a baking tray under a hot grill until blistered and blackened. Remove them from beneath the grill and allow to cool down. When cool enough to handle, peel off the skin and chop the flesh into small pieces.

2. Heat the olive oil in a large saucepan over a medium heat, add the onion, celery and garlic and cook until the onion is softened but not browned.

3. Add the water, vegetable stock, tomatoes, black-eyed beans, sweet potato and sweet red pepper. Next add the sugar and all the seasonings with the exception of the salt and pepper. Stir thoroughly and bring the mixture to a boil. Reduce the heat, cover, and simmer for about 20 minutes or until the sweet potatoes are soft.

4. Season the soup to taste and then leave it to cool. Pour it into a large bowl, cover, and refrigerate for at least 4 hours.

5. Serve in individual bowls with chopped fresh parsley sprinkled over each one.

VARIATION

1 onion, roughly chopped
1 red chilli, finely chopped
2 garlic cloves, crushed
1 tsp ground coriander
30g/1oz butter
450g/1lb sweet potatoes,
    peeled and cut into
    chunks
500ml/16fl oz vegetable stock
75g/2½oz Gruyère cheese,
    grated, to garnish

Fry the onion, chilli, garlic and coriander in the butter until soft. Add the sweet potatoes and stock, bring to the boil then simmer until the potatoes are soft. Blend, season and chill. Serve garnished with cheese.

SQUASH, SPLIT PEA & PRAWN SOUP

This enchanting combination of flavours is delicious and can be served as a summer cooler at any time.

INGREDIENTS *Serves 6*

450g/1lb yellow squash flesh, diced

1 tsp olive oil

¼ tsp salt

¼ tsp ground black pepper

60g/2oz butter

1 onion, chopped

1 litre/1¾ pints chicken stock (see p.12)

120ml/4fl oz dry white wine

175g/6oz raw prawns, shelled

1 lemon grass stalk

1 tsp ground cumin

½ tsp ground turmeric

225g/8oz dried yellow split peas

120ml/4fl oz whipping cream

METHOD

1. Preheat the oven to 200°C/400°F/gas mark 6.

2. Toss the squash in the olive oil with the salt and pepper and arrange in a single layer on a baking tray. Bake in the oven for 15–20 minutes or until the squash is tender.

3. Melt the butter in a large saucepan over a medium heat and add the onion. Sauté for 8–10 minutes until soft but not brown, stirring occasionally.

4. Add the stock and wine and bring to a slow boil. Reduce the heat, add the prawns and simmer, uncovered, until they are pink on the outside and opaque. Remove the prawns with a slotted spoon and put them into a clean bowl. Set aside in the refrigerator.

5. Rinse the lemon grass stalk under cold water and cut off the tough top and root. Crush the tender inner stalk with a mallet and add to the saucepan, together with the cumin, turmeric and split peas.

6. Bring the soup back to the boil, then cover and reduce the heat until just simmering. Cook for about 50–60 minutes or until the peas are soft and cooked.

7. Stir in the roasted squash, reserving about one-third for garnish. Pour the soup into a blender and process until thick and smooth.

8. Pour the soup into a clean bowl, add the cream and taste for seasoning. Adjust as necessary. Cover and chill for at least 4 hours or overnight.

9. When you are ready to serve, divide the prawns between 6 bowls and ladle the soup over the top. Garnish the soup with the reserved roasted squash. If you are serving this at a dinner party, surprise your guests by also garnishing the soup with vibrant nasturtium flowers.

NASTURTIUMS

Nasturtiums were first discovered in the 16th century deep in the forests of Peru. As well as acting as a decorative flower and a companion plant in the organic garden, they have many culinary uses. The flowers can be used in soups, as decoration, in salads, to flavour vinegars or in a fragrant butter – try the recipe below:

250g/9oz butter
20 nasturtium flower heads, finely chopped
2 tbsp fresh chives, chopped
salt and pepper to taste

Put all the ingredients in a bowl and blend well with a fork. Use the butter on mixed vegetables or on seafood. Substitute cream cheese for butter, if preferred.

SWEETCORN SOUP

An ingenious mixture of flavours – sweetness from the onion,
creaminess from the sweetcorn and heat from the chilli.

INGREDIENTS *Serves 4–6*

10 sweetcorn cobs
30g/1oz unsalted butter
2 onions, finely chopped
1 potato, peeled and chopped
1 litre/1¾ pints vegetable stock
   (see p.14)
salt and freshly ground black
   pepper, to taste
1 roasted large red chilli,
   to garnish

METHOD

1. Using the largest holes on a
hand grater, grate off the corn
kernels into a large bowl and
set aside.
2. Melt the butter in a large
saucepan over a medium heat
and sauté the onion for about
3 minutes or until it starts to soften
but not colour.
3. Add the chopped potato and
vegetable stock to the pan and

bring to the boil. Reduce the heat
to a gentle simmer and cook for
about 10–15 minutes or until the
potato is soft.
4. Add the corn kernels and cook
for a further 2 minutes.
5. Pour into a blender and
process until you have a smooth,
creamy consistency.
6. Transfer the soup to a large
bowl and taste for seasoning,
adding salt and pepper as
necessary. Cover the bowl
and chill in the refrigerator
for 2–3 hours.
7. Place the chilli under a hot
grill until the skin starts to blister
and char. When cool, chop it
into tiny pieces. Sprinkle a few
pieces onto each bowl of soup as
you serve.

VICHYSSOISE

Believed to have been created in the early 20th century, vichyssoise is a creamy potato and leek soup designed to cool the body rapidly in the summer heat.

INGREDIENTS *Serves 4*

60g/2oz unsalted butter

1 onion, chopped

300g/10oz leeks, finely sliced

1 tbsp dry white wine

115g/4oz potatoes, peeled and
   diced

300ml/10fl oz chicken stock
   (see p.12)

300ml/10fl oz whole milk

2 tbsp double cream

salt and freshly ground black
   pepper, to taste

TO GARNISH:

1 tbsp snipped chives

1 tbsp chopped fresh parsley

1 tsp sweet paprika

METHOD

1. Melt the butter in a large saucepan over a medium heat. Add the onion and leeks and cook for about 10–15 minutes or until softened.

2. Add the wine, potatoes and stock and bring to the boil. Reduce the heat so that the stock is simmering and cook for about 15–20 minutes or until the potatoes are soft.

3. Pour the soup into a blender and process until you have a smooth purée. Pass the soup through a fine sieve into a large bowl, add the milk and cream and season to taste with salt and pepper.

4. Cover the bowl, put it in the refrigerator and chill for at least 2 hours or until you are ready to serve.

5. Serve in individual bowls garnished with the chives, parsley and a little sprinkle of sweet paprika.

WATERCRESS & SPINACH SOUP

The peppery flavour of the watercress adds an extra punch to this vibrant green soup.

INGREDIENTS *Serves 4*

60g/2oz unsalted butter
1 large onion, chopped
2 young celery sticks, diced
1 garlic clove, finely chopped
1 leek, white parts only, thinly
  sliced
1 potato, peeled and diced
750ml/1¼ pints vegetable stock
  (see p.14)
150g/5½oz baby spinach leaves
170g/6oz watercress, coarsely
  chopped
175g/6oz frozen peas
150ml/5fl oz double cream
1 tsp lemon juice
salt and freshly ground black
  pepper, to taste

TO GARNISH:

2 hard-boiled eggs, chopped
1 tbsp snipped chives
small watercress sprigs

METHOD

1. Melt the butter in a large saucepan over a medium heat. Add the onion, celery, garlic, leek and potato and cook for about 10–15 minutes or until the vegetables have softened but not browned.

2. Add the stock and bring to the boil. Reduce the heat and simmer, covered, for 15–20 minutes or until the vegetables are very soft. Add the spinach, watercress and peas, and cook until the spinach has wilted.

3. Purée the soup in a blender, then transfer to a large bowl. Allow to cool before pouring in the cream and seasoning to taste with lemon juice and salt and pepper. Chill for at least 2 hours in the refrigerator before serving in individual bowls with the various garnishes.

PART 6

FRUITY SUMMER SOUPS

We tend to think of soup as a dish made of vegetables, meat or fish. But there are many different types. This section features some less conventional soups, consisting just of fruit or with fruit as an addition. They make a delicious light meal and can be just as satisfying as the more traditional types.

MAKING FRUIT SOUPS

Many of the recipes for fruit soups are designed to use up a glut of fruit during the summer months. Tantalizing and refreshing, they may be consumed hot or cold, spicy or sweet, and can be made extra-special with the addition of a little alcohol.

Soups made from fruit, or with the addition of fruit, can be served as a starter, a main course or even a dessert. They may be thickened and embellished with the addition of cream, yogurt or even your favourite liqueur or champagne. If served as a dessert, they can be topped with crispy little circles of puff pastry or cubes of sponge cake dusted with icing sugar.

As some fruits have a muddy appearance when combined – red and green, for example – care needs to be taken to ensure the colour of the soup looks palatable.

Choose only ripe, really fresh fruit and experiment with mixing different flavours. Make sure the fruit you use is not bruised or starting to wither, as this will impair the taste. Fruits such as strawberries, peaches, apples and apricots all make a good base to which other flavours can be added. Some fruit, such as apple, goes brown very quickly once it has been peeled and cut, so be sure to place apple slices in water with the juice of a lemon to stop them discolouring.

If you prepare your fruit in advance, do not store it in the refrigerator for more than an hour ahead of cooking as it will start to lose its natural sweetness.

Fresh herbs – mint, in particular – go well with fruit soups, so be sure to keep some handy. Try growing a few on your windowsill.

APPLE SOUP

This soup is excellent served as a dessert in pretty little glass bowls or as a starter to a main course containing pork.

INGREDIENTS *Serves 4–6*
600ml/1 pint water
115g/4oz sugar
5 large cooking apples, peeled,
    cored and sliced
500ml/16fl oz white wine
    (preferably Riesling)
grated zest of 1 lemon
1 cinnamon stick
2 tbsp apricot jam
3 tbsp fresh white breadcrumbs
juice of ½ lemon
crème fraîche and 1 eating
    apple, peeled and sliced,
    to serve

METHOD
1. Bring the water to the boil in a large saucepan, add the sugar and stir until it has dissolved.
2. Add the apples, wine, lemon zest and cinnamon stick and bring back to the boil. Reduce the heat, cover, and simmer for about 15 minutes or until the apples are soft but not pulpy.
3. Stir in the jam, breadcrumbs and lemon juice and simmer for another 10 minutes.
4. Remove the cinnamon stick and allow the soup to cool, then pour into a blender and process until smooth. Pour into a bowl, cover and chill. Serve with some crème fraîche and a few slices of apple in each bowl.

APRICOT SOUP

This makes a wonderful starter or a lovely finish to a meal if swirled with soured cream and garnished with crumbled amaretti biscuits.

INGREDIENTS *Serves 4*
450g/1lb apricots
750ml/1¼ pints water
60g/2oz sugar
1 tbsp lemon juice
1 tsp grated lemon zest
1 tbsp cornflour

TO GARNISH:
2 tbsp soured cream
crushed amaretti biscuits

METHOD

1. Halve the apricots, reserving the stones. Tie the stones in a piece of clean muslin and secure tightly.

2. Put the apricots and muslin bag into a large saucepan with the water and bring to the boil. Reduce the heat and simmer for 20–30 minutes, partially covered, until the apricots are soft.

3. Remove the muslin bag, then pour the liquid into a blender and process until you have a smooth, silky texture.

4. Return the liquid to a clean saucepan, stir in the sugar and lemon juice and zest and bring it back to boiling point.

5. Mix the cornflour with a little water to make a smooth paste and stir it into the hot soup. Simmer over a low heat for several minutes or until the soup is clear and thick.

6. If you want to serve the soup cold, pour it into a bowl, cover, allow to cool then chill in the refrigerator for 4 hours. Serve with a swirl of soured cream and a sprinkling of crushed biscuits on top of each bowl.

7. If you want to serve this as a hot soup, simply ladle it into bowls and swirl some soured cream on top.

BANANA SOUP

This recipe originated in the Caribbean. The subtle infusion of sweet and savoury flavours makes it irresistible.

INGREDIENTS Serves 2

30g/1oz unsalted butter
1 shallot, finely chopped
1 banana, sliced
2.5cm/1in fresh root ginger, grated
60g/2oz basmati rice
2 lime leaves, bruised
½ tsp curry powder
½ tsp ground cinnamon
400ml/14fl oz chicken stock (see p.14)
2 tbsp coconut cream
150ml/5fl oz plain yogurt

METHOD

1. Melt the butter in a large saucepan over a medium heat and add the shallot. Sauté until the shallot is translucent but not browned.

2. Add the banana, ginger, rice and all the spices. Pour the stock into the pan and bring to the boil. Reduce the heat and simmer for 20 minutes, covered, or until the rice is cooked.

3. Allow to cool slightly, remove the lime leaves, then pour into a blender. Add the coconut cream and process until you have a rich, velvety texture.

4. Pour the soup into a bowl and add the yogurt. If you find the soup is too thick at this stage, add a little water and stir to combine.

5. Serve as a starter or a light lunch, either warm or chilled, with a slice of brown bread.

CHEF'S TIP

Don't reheat the soup after you have added the yogurt or it will curdle.

CHERRY SOUP

This special-occasion soup is enlivened with champagne to complement the sweet-sour cherries.

INGREDIENTS *Serves 4*
900g/2lb red cherries
1 cinnamon stick
3 whole cloves
250ml/8fl oz water
500ml/16fl oz champagne
1 vanilla pod, split
115g/4oz sugar
75ml/2½fl oz freshly squeezed
   orange juice
1 tbsp lemon juice
grated zest of 1 orange
2 tbsp crème fraîche and 4 sprigs
   of mint, to garnish

METHOD

1. Stone the cherries, then put the stones in a piece of clean muslin with the cinnamon stick and cloves and secure firmly. Hit the muslin bag with a hammer to break the stones.

2. Put two-thirds of the cherries into a large saucepan and add the muslin bag, water, champagne, vanilla pod and sugar. Bring to the boil, stirring until the sugar has dissolved, then reduce the heat and simmer for about 25–30 minutes or until the cherries are very soft.

3. Remove the muslin bag and vanilla pod, then pour the soup into a blender and purée until smooth.

4. Return the soup to the saucepan and add the muslin bag, the remaining cherries, the orange and lemon juice and the orange zest. Cook on a low heat until the cherries start to soften. Remove the muslin bag and pour the soup into a large bowl. Once cool, place in the refrigerator for 3–4 hours to chill thoroughly.

5. Serve with a pool of crème fraîche and a little sprig of mint in the centre of each bowl.

CUCUMBER & APPLE SOUP

This is a beautiful pale green, refreshing soup to serve chilled at the height of summer. Although it is a savoury soup it is packed full of fruit flavours.

INGREDIENTS *Serves 4*

1 tbsp olive oil

2 shallots, chopped

4 cucumbers, peeled, deseeded and chopped

375ml/13fl oz vegetable stock (see p.14)

115g/4oz seedless white grapes

2 eating apples, peeled, cored and diced

1 tbsp chopped fresh mint leaves

250ml/8fl oz buttermilk or soured cream

salt and freshly ground black pepper, to taste

METHOD

1. Heat the oil in a small saucepan over a medium heat and add the shallots. Cook for about 5 minutes or until the shallots are translucent but not browned. Remove the pan from the heat and allow to cool.

2. Put the shallots into a blender together with all the remaining ingredients except the salt and pepper and process until the soup is a smooth consistency.

3. Pour the soup into a large bowl and season to taste with salt and pepper. Cover and chill in the refrigerator for 3–4 hours before serving.

MANGO & MELON SOUP

This recipe for mango soup is so simple that it doesn't require any cooking at all.

INGREDIENTS *Serves 4–6*

2 mangoes, peeled, stoned
  and chopped
350g/12oz cantaloupe melon,
  peeled, deseeded and
  chopped
2 tbsp fresh mint, finely chopped
2 tbsp fresh lemon juice
1 tbsp icing sugar
75ml/2½fl oz dry white wine
2 tbsp plain yogurt
tiny mint leaves, to garnish

METHOD

1. Put all the ingredients except
the mint into a blender and
process to a smooth consistency.
Serve garnished with mint
leaves.

Try serving this and any other
fruit soup with thin vanilla wafers
(see right).

VANILLA WAFERS

225g/8oz butter, softened
450g/1lb sugar
2 tbsp vanilla extract
250g/9oz plain flour
1 tsp baking powder
½ tsp salt
2 eggs, beaten

Cream the butter and sugar
in a bowl with the vanilla
extract. Mix together the
dry ingredients and add
them to the bowl. Beat in
the eggs. Drop tablespoons
of the batter 5cm/2in apart
onto a baking tray. Bake at
180°C/350°F/gas mark 4 for
15 minutes until golden.

MELON & STRAWBERRY SOUP

This sophisticated soup is perfect served as a palate cleanser between courses.

INGREDIENTS *Serves 4*

1 small canteloupe melon, peeled, deseeded and cut into 2.5cm/1in cubes

1 tbsp maple syrup

1 tbsp water

280g/10oz fresh strawberries, hulled

½ tsp balsamic vinegar

1cm/½in fresh root ginger, grated

fresh raspberries, to garnish

METHOD

1. Put the melon, maple syrup and water into a blender and process until smooth. Pour into a bowl, cover and refrigerate.

2. Wash the bowl of the blender, then purée the strawberries with the balsamic vinegar and ginger. Pass through a fine sieve, discarding any solids, then pour into a bowl, cover and refrigerate.

3. When you are ready to serve, divide the melon purée between chilled glasses. Pour the strawberry purée into the centre of the melon purée and then swirl gently to partially combine the two. Top each glass with the chilled raspberries.

NECTARINE SOUP

This is good served chilled or you can use it to accompany spicy barbecued chicken or corn on the cob.

INGREDIENTS *Serves 4*
675g/1½lb ripe nectarines, stoned
    and chopped
250ml/8fl oz freshly squeezed
    orange juice
120ml/4fl oz dry white wine
¼ tsp Tabasco sauce
½ tbsp balsamic vinegar
2 tbsp fresh coriander leaves,
    plus extra for garnish

METHOD
1. Put the nectarines, orange juice, wine, Tabasco sauce and balsamic vinegar into a blender and process until smooth. Add the coriander and pulse until it is chopped into the soup.
2. Put the soup into a large bowl and chill in the refrigerator until required.
3. Serve in individual bowls with a few small coriander leaves on the top of each one.

CHEF'S TIP

If you don't have the time to chill your fruit soup in the refrigerator, simply add a few ice cubes to the blender when you process it.

ORANGE SOUP

Delicately sweet, but with a slight bite, this light soup makes an excellent starter on a summer's evening.

INGREDIENTS Serves 4

115g/4oz sugar
500ml/16fl oz water
1 cinnamon stick
pared zest of 1 orange
250ml/8fl oz freshly squeezed
    orange juice
250ml/8fl oz sweet white wine
4 oranges, peeled and
    segmented, with all
    membrane and
    seeds removed

METHOD

1. Bring the sugar, water, cinnamon stick and orange zest to the boil in a large saucepan. Reduce the heat to medium and cook for about 10–15 minutes or until the mixture is syrupy.

2. Remove from the heat and add the orange juice and wine, stirring to combine. Remove the orange zest and cinnamon stick, then transfer the soup to a bowl to chill for a couple of hours.

3. When you are ready to serve, divide the orange segments between 4 serving bowls and pour in the chilled orange soup. There is no need to add any garnish – the flavours are just perfect on their own.

CHEF'S TIP

This soup can also be made with sweet mandarins, which are generally available in the supermarkets between November and April. They have a distinctive flavour and are very easy to peel and segment.

ORANGE & TOMATO SOUP

If you like the flavour of oranges, try this combination for a savoury summer soup that can be served either hot or chilled.

INGREDIENTS *Serves 4*

30g/1oz unsalted butter

2 onions, chopped

3 garlic cloves, finely chopped

3 tbsp plain flour

900g/2lb ripe tomatoes, skinned
   and chopped

1.2 litres/2 pints vegetable stock
   (see p.14)

250ml/8fl oz freshly squeezed
   orange juice

pared zest of 1 orange

2 tsp sugar

½ tsp Tabasco sauce

salt and freshly ground black
   pepper, to taste

fresh basil leaves, finely chopped

METHOD

1. Melt the butter in a large saucepan over a medium heat. Add the chopped onions and garlic and cook for 5–6 minutes until the onions have softened and are translucent but not browned.

2. Stir in the flour and cook for a further minute. Add the chopped tomatoes and cook for 2 minutes, stirring continuously.

3. Add the stock, orange juice and pared orange zest. Bring to the boil, then reduce the heat and simmer, covered, for 15 minutes, stirring occasionally.

4. Add the sugar and Tabasco sauce, stir, then remove from the heat and allow to cool slightly.

5. Pour the soup into a blender and process until smooth. Taste and season with salt and pepper. Pour the soup into a bowl and chill for 2–3 hours or until you are ready to serve.

6. Serve in individual bowls garnished with chopped basil leaves. For a spicier flavour, sprinkle with a few chilli flakes.

PEACH SOUP WITH ALMONDS

This soup has a subtle, sweet flavour and is the colour of sunshine on a plate. For optimum flavour, make sure you use only the ripest and juiciest peaches.

INGREDIENTS *Serves 4–6*

900g/2lb peaches, peeled, stoned
   and sliced
250ml/8fl oz freshly squeezed
   orange juice
250ml/8fl oz peach juice
60ml/2fl oz lime juice
2 tbsp runny honey
1 tsp ground ginger
¼ tsp ground cardamon
¼ tsp ground cinnamon
2 whole cloves
120ml/4fl oz plain yogurt
2 tbsp amaretto liqueur
75g/2½oz flaked almonds,
   toasted, to garnish

METHOD

1. In a large saucepan, combine the peaches, orange, peach and lime juices, honey, ginger, cardamon, cinnamon and cloves. Bring the mixture to a boil, stir, then reduce the heat. Cover the pan and simmer for about 12–15 minutes or until the peaches are soft. Leave to cool and remove the cloves.

2. Pour the soup into a blender and process until smooth.

3. Pour the soup into a bowl, stir in the yogurt and amaretto, cover, and refrigerate for at least 4 hours.

4. Serve in individual bowls sprinkled with the toasted flaked almonds.

PEAR SOUP

The delicate flavour of pears with a hint of sage makes
this soup a lovely light starter.

INGREDIENTS *Serves 4*

6 pears, peeled, cored and
   halved
3 tbsp freshly squeezed
   lemon juice
60g/2oz unsalted butter
2 tsp finely chopped fresh
   sage leaves
115g/4oz light brown sugar
120ml/4fl oz water

METHOD

1. Prepare the pears and toss
them in the lemon juice to
prevent them going brown.
2. Heat the butter in a large
saucepan until it turns slightly
brown. Add the sage and cook
until it starts to caramelize. Add
the sugar and stir until dissolved.
3. Drain the pears, add them to
the pan and roll them around
so they are thoroughly coated
in the sugar mixture. Cook over

medium heat for 15 minutes or
until they are light brown.
4. Put the pear mixture into
a blender with the water and
process until smooth. Serve the
soup either warm or chilled.

VARIATION

For a change, replace the
sage leaves with a fennel
bulb, cored and chopped.
Add the fennel instead of
the sage during Step 2.
Cook for about 5–8 minutes
or until the fennel has
softened and is starting to
caramelize. Proceed with
the remaining steps of the
recipe as before.

PEAR & BRIE SOUP

This is a beautifully indulgent soup which should be eaten slowly so that every mouthful is savoured. If you like a slightly stronger flavour, substitute cambozola cheese for the brie.

INGREDIENTS *Serves 4*

75ml/2½fl oz unsalted butter
3 onions, chopped
1 garlic clove, finely chopped
8 ripe pears, peeled, cored
    and sliced
250ml/8fl oz white wine
1.2 litres/2 pints vegetable stock
    (see p.14)
225g/8oz ripe brie cheese, rind
    removed, softened to room
    temperature
250ml/8fl oz double cream
salt and freshly ground black
    pepper, to taste
violet flowers and snipped
    chives, to garnish

METHOD

1. Melt the butter in a large saucepan over a medium heat and stir in the onions, garlic and pears. Sauté for about 5 minutes or until the onion is soft but not browned.

2. Deglaze the pan with the wine, then stir in the vegetable stock. Bring to the boil, reduce the heat and simmer for 1 hour, covered.

3. Chop the cheese into cubes and stir it into the soup until completely melted.

4. Whisk in the cream and season the soup with salt and pepper. Pour into a large bowl, cover and chill in the refrigerator for at least 2 hours before serving.

5. Stir well before serving and garnish with a few violet petals and snipped chives.

You might also like to make some walnut bread, which is a perfect accompaniment to this delicious soup.

PLUM SOUP

This is a good soup to serve at Christmas as it has all the lovely warming flavours of mulled wine.

INGREDIENTS *Serves 4*

90ml/3fl oz port

1 cinnamon stick

2 whole cloves

5 black peppercorns

peel of 1 orange

1kg/2¼lb ripe plums, stoned and quartered

200ml/7fl oz good-quality red wine

2½ tbsp icing sugar

200ml/7fl oz tub of mascarpone cheese

¼ tsp cinnamon

the juice of ½ orange

1 small panettone, cut into thick slices, to serve

METHOD

1. Put the port, cinnamon stick, cloves, peppercorns and orange peel in a large saucepan and bring to the boil. Reduce the heat and cook until the mixture is the consistency of syrup.

2. Add the plums and squash them down into the syrup. Pour the red wine over and stir in 1 tablespoon of icing sugar. Bring to the boil, then turn the heat down to a gentle simmer. Cover and cook for about 25–30 minutes or until the plums have cooked down to a purée. Taste and adjust the sweetness if necessary.

3. Pass the soup through a fine sieve, discarding any solids.

4. Mix the mascarpone cheese with the cinnamon and 2 teaspoons of icing sugar. Add the orange juice and mix to a smooth consistency.

5. Serve the soup chilled, with a spoonful of mascarpone in the centre. Sprinkle the panettone slices with icing sugar and put them under a hot grill until slightly browned.

RASPBERRY SOUP

This is probably one of the easiest soups you will ever make, yet also one of the most impressive. It is a hit with all ages and can be served as a starter before a barbecue or as a light dessert.

INGREDIENTS *Serves 4*

250g/9oz fresh raspberries
600ml/1 pint water
115g/4oz sugar
1 tsp lemon juice
1 tsp vanilla extract
3 tbsp tapioca
fresh raspberries and strips of
   lemon zest, to garnish

METHOD

1. In a medium saucepan, bring the raspberries, water, sugar and lemon juice to the boil, stirring, until the sugar is completely dissolved.
2. Allow the mixture to cool slightly, then strain it through a fine sieve lined with muslin. Discard any solids.
3. Put the soup into a clean pan and add the vanilla extract and tapioca. Cook over a medium heat until the soup has thickened. Leave to cool to room temperature.
4. Pour the soup into a bowl, cover and chill for at least 2 hours or until ready to serve.
5. Serve in bowls garnished with a few fresh raspberries and slivers of lemon zest.

VARIATION

After you have strained the soup through the muslin, add 250ml/8fl oz of plain yogurt and substitute 3 tablespoons of honey for the sugar and orange for the lemon juice. Omit the tapioca and do not reheat.

REDCURRANT SOUP

This recipe started out as an experiment with a glut of redcurrants, but the result was so good that it deserves a place in this section.

INGREDIENTS *Serves 4*
400g/14oz redcurrants
5cm/2in cinnamon stick
2 whole cloves
2 slices of lemon
200g/7oz sugar
750ml/1¼ pints water
1½ tbsp freshly squeezed
    lemon juice
1 tbsp cornflour
1 tbsp water
double cream, to garnish

METHOD
1. Put the redcurrants, cinnamon stick, cloves, lemon slices, sugar and water into a large saucepan and bring to the boil. Reduce the heat, cover and simmer for about 15 minutes or until the redcurrants are very soft.
2. Remove the lemon slices, cinnamon and cloves, pour the mixture into a blender and process until very smooth.
3. Pass the purée through a fine sieve and discard any seeds, then pour it into a clean saucepan and add the lemon juice.
4. Combine the cornflour with the water until smooth, then gradually add this mixture to the saucepan, stirring continuously. Continue to stir while you bring the soup to near boiling point or until it has cleared and thickened.
5. Allow the soup to cool, then pour it into a large bowl. Cover and chill in the refrigerator for at least 2 hours before serving.
6. Serve the soup in individual bowls with a swirl of double cream in each. This soup can be enjoyed either as a starter or a dessert.

RHUBARB SOUP

A lovely way to prepare rhubarb, this pretty pink soup is delicate and refreshes the palate.

INGREDIENTS *Serves 4*
500ml/16fl oz water
225g/8oz rhubarb, cut into bite-
 sized chunks
115g/4oz sugar
1 cinnamon stick
2 tbsp cornflour
2 tbsp water
whipped cream, to garnish

METHOD

1. Bring the water to the boil in a large saucepan, then add the rhubarb, sugar and cinnamon stick. Reduce the heat, cover and simmer for 15 minutes or until the rhubarb is very tender.

2. Mix the cornflour with the water and slowly stir it into the hot soup. Stir until it is completely combined, then cook for several minutes or until the soup is clear and thickened.

3. Remove the cinnamon stick and leave the soup to cool slightly. Pour it into a large bowl, then cover and chill in the refrigerator for 2–3 hours or until ready to serve.

4. Ladle the soup into individual bowls and float a spoonful of whipped cream on the surface.

CHEF'S TIP

To prepare the rhubarb, first remove the leaves, then rinse the stalks and pat them dry. Trim the ends and cut the rhubarb into chunks. If you find the stalks have tough strings running through them, simply pull these out with your fingers.

STRAWBERRY SOUP I

Strawberries are one of the most delectable fruits available and can be prepared in so many ways. They make the most amazing summer soups. The second recipe here is for adults only!

INGREDIENTS *Serves 4*
675g/1½lb fresh strawberries,
   hulled
450ml/15fl oz natural yogurt
120ml/4fl oz freshly squeezed
   orange juice
115g/4oz caster sugar

⅛ tsp ground cardamon

METHOD
1. Combine all the ingredients in a blender and process until you have a fine purée. Mix well and serve chilled.

STRAWBERRY SOUP II

INGREDIENTS *Serves 4*
300ml/10fl oz red wine
200g/7oz icing sugar
2 tbsp brandy
400g/14oz fresh
   strawberries, hulled

and simmer until the volume has reduced by half.
2. Purée the strawberries in a blender and fold them into the wine mixture. Pour into a bowl and chill in the refrigerator for 2 hours.

METHOD
1. Heat the wine, icing sugar and brandy in a medium saucepan until boiling. Reduce the heat

This soup is delectable served with crushed meringues sprinkled on top.

STRAWBERRY BALSAMIC SOUP

Balsamic vinegar and strawberries complement each other perfectly. You might like to keep your guests guessing as to the secret ingredient here!

INGREDIENTS *Serves 4*

900g/2lb fresh strawberries, hulled, some reserved for garnish

225g/8oz caster sugar

6 tbsp balsamic vinegar

1 tsp grated orange zest

½ tsp grated lemon zest

1 tbsp freshly squeezed orange juice

500ml/16fl oz natural yogurt

icing sugar and fanned strawberries, to garnish (see right)

CHEF'S TIP

Impress your guests with some fanned strawberries. Place each strawberry on a cutting board, pointed end facing you. Using a sharp knife, make 5 cuts lengthways, stopping just short of the stem end. Fan the slices apart, keeping them attached at the base.

METHOD

1. Put all the ingredients except the yogurt into a blender and process until smooth. Leave to stand for 5 minutes, stirring occasionally, to make sure the sugar has dissolved completely.

2. Pour the strawberry purée into a large bowl and stir in the yogurt until smooth. Cover the bowl and chill for 2 hours before serving.

3. Sift some icing sugar over the fanned strawberries and add a couple to each bowl of soup.

STRAWBERRY & PEACH SOUP

Here is another intoxicating combination of flavours –
the true taste of summer in a bowl.

INGREDIENTS *Serves 4*
4 large peaches, stoned and cut
   into chunks (with skin)
3 fresh rosemary sprigs
juice of 1 lemon
115g/4oz sugar
½ tsp ground cinnamon
750ml/1¼ pints water
175g/6oz strawberries, hulled
plain yogurt or whipped cream,
   to garnish

METHOD
1. Place the prepared peaches in
a large saucepan.
2. Tie the rosemary sprigs inside
a piece of clean muslin and
secure firmly.
3. Add the muslin to the
saucepan together with the
lemon juice, sugar, cinnamon

and water. Bring to the boil, then
reduce the heat and simmer
gently, covered, for about 20
minutes or until the peaches
are soft.
4. Purée the strawberries in a
blender, then pass through a fine
sieve, discarding any flesh and
seeds. Set aside.
5. Strain the peaches, discarding
the muslin bag and reserving
the cooking liquid. Purée the
peaches in the blender. Add half
the liquid to the peach purée and
process for a further 30 seconds.
6. Transfer the peach purée
to a large bowl and stir in the
remaining liquid. Cover and
chill in the refrigerator, stirring
occasionally, for about 1 hour.
7. When thoroughly chilled,
whisk in the strawberry purée
and serve with some plain yogurt
or whipped cream.

WATERMELON SOUP

This outstanding soup has added honey and lime to give it an extra-special zing. Serve decorated with little melon balls and some frosted mint leaves.

INGREDIENTS *Serves 4*

600g/1lb 5oz watermelon, peeled, deseeded and cut into cubes
75ml/2½fl oz pure apple juice
2 tbsp freshly squeezed lime juice
1 tsp finely chopped fresh mint
½ tsp ground ginger
2 tsp runny honey
60ml/2fl oz natural yogurt

METHOD

1. Put the watermelon, apple juice, lime juice, mint and ginger into a blender and process until smooth, stopping occasionally to scrape the sides of the bowl. Transfer to a bowl, cover and chill for at least 1 hour.

2. Taste and add honey if needed – the melon may be sweet enough already. Serve in individual bowls with a spoonful of yogurt on top.

FROSTED MINT LEAVES

3 dozen mint leaves
1 egg white
icing sugar

Select only perfect mint leaves and wash them carefully. Dry with kitchen paper. Beat the egg white in a small bowl until it starts to foam. Spread a thick layer of icing sugar on a piece of greaseproof paper. Use a pastry brush to coat each side of the leaves lightly with egg white, then dip them in the sugar. Leave to dry at room temperature for 2 hours.

INDEX